THE MARCH OF THE MILLENNIA

THE MARCH OF THE MILLENNIA: *A Key to Looking at History*

7000 B.C.
Irrigation begins

5000 B.C.
Priest-kings become city-state rulers
World population at 5 million

4000 B.C.
City of Ur founded
Metallurgy invented
World population at 7 million

8000 B.C.
World population at 4 million
Agriculture invented
Organized warfare begins
Cities appear
Beginning of civilization

6000 B.C.
Pottery developed
Textiles developed

Sumerians enter Tigris-Euphrates Valley
City-states dominant political form

3000 B.C.
Bronze Age

628 B.C.
Birth of Zarathustra, founder of Zoroastrianism

670 B.C.
Birth of Solon, first "legislator," and early developer of democracy

753 B.C.
Founding of Rome

625 B.C.
Birth of Thales of Miletus, first natural philosopher

630 B.C.
Nebuchadnezzar's Rule of Chaldean Empire begins

680 B.C.
Lydians invent coins

586 B.C.
Temple of Jerusalem destroyed

565 B.C.
Taoism appears in China

550 B.C.
Cyrus creates new Persian Empire

585 B.C.
Eclipse of May 28; first event in history known to exact day of occurrence

563 B.C.
Birth of Siddharta Gautama (The Buddha) in India

509 B.C.
Romans overthrow Etruscan monarchy

A.D. 135
Jewish "Diaspora" begins

A.D. 9
Roman defeat in Teutoberg Forest puts Empire on defensive

27 B.C.
Octavian (Caesar Augustus) becomes emperor of Rome

A.D. 70
Jews' revolt against Rome is crushed; Temple destroyed

1 B.C./A.D. 1
World population at 170 million
Birth of Jesus (approximate date)

A.D. 410
Rome sacked by Visigoths

A.D. 476
Fall of Roman Empire in the West; Dark Age begins in Europe

A.D. 570
Birth of Muhammad, founder of Islam

A.D. 306
Constantine I becomes Roman Emperor; "Christianizes" the Empire

A.D. 451
Attila the Hun defeated

A.D. 540
Gregory I establishes modern Papacy

Wheels first used for
    transportation
Writing invented by Sumerians
Egypt united into first nation-
    state
World population at 14 million

Great Pyramid of Cheops built
2530 B.C.

Indus River civilization in India
    at its peak
World population at 27 million
2000 B.C.

2800 B.C.
Great Flood in Tigris-Euphrates
    Valley

2340 B.C.
Akkadians enter Tigris-
    Euphrates Valley
Sargon creates first empire

1728 B.C.
Reign of Hammurabi begins;
    written law code developed

Greece and Tigris-Euphrates
    Valley enter Dark Age
Phoenicians invent alphabet
China's population at 5 million
1000 B.C.

Hittites initiate Iron Age
Iron Age
1300 B.C.

China enters Bronze Age
Aryans invade India
Eruption of Thera; decline of
    Cretan civilization
1500 B.C.

962 B.C.
Reign of Solomon begins

1200 B.C.
Siege of Troy

1379 B.C.
Reign of Akhenaton begins in
    Egypt

1720 B.C.
Charioteers conquer Egypt

Greeks defeat Persians at
    Marathon
490 B.C.

Peloponnesian War begins
431 B.C.

Birth of Aristotle
384 B.C.

Seleucid Era
330 B.C.

460 B.C.
Golden Age
Pericles rules Athens

428 B.C.
Birth of Plato

334 B.C.
Alexander the Great begins his
    conquests

Julius Caesar assassinated
44 B.C.

Rome destroys Carthage
146 B.C.

India unified
321 B.C.

130 B.C.
Rome become leading power of
    Mediterranean

250 B.C.
Bible translated into Greek

323 B.C.
Death of Alexander the Great

China most advanced region of the
    world, with population of 60
    million
World population at 265 million

Schism between Roman
    Catholic and Greek
    Orthodox churches
A.D. 1054

Charlemagne crowned Emperor
A.D. 800

A.D. 732
Charles Martel defeats Moors
    at Battle of Tours

A.D. 1000
Otto I rules Holy Roman
    Empire
Byzantine (East Roman)
    Empire at its peak

A.D. 1066
England conquered by William
    I of Normandy

THE MARCH OF THE MILLENNIA: *A Key to Looking at History*

A.D. 1210
Kublai Khan rules China

A.D. 1300
Europeans gain knowledge of gunpowder and magnetic compass from China

A.D. 1096
Crusades begin; Europeans come into contact with other cultures and rediscover ancient knowledge

A.D. 1204
Crusaders sack Constantinople

A.D. 1240
Mongols invade Europe

A.D. 1666
Isaac Newton formulates the theory of universal gravitation

A.D. 1620
Plymouth Colony established in New World

A.D. 1603
Shogunate established in Japan

A.D. 1688
"Glorious Revolution" brings limited monarchical rule to England

A.D. 1643
Reign of Louis XIV begins in France

A.D. 1609
Galileo uses telescope to discover moons of Jupiter

A.D. 1765
Industrial Revolution begins with invention of steam engine by James Watt

A.D. 1776
American Declaration of Independence

A.D. 1689
Peter the Great attempts to Westernize Russia

A.D. 1765
Industrial Revolution

A.D. 1783
American colonies defeat British

A.D. 1947
India becomes independent and is partitioned
Creation of Israel

A.D. 1941
Japan attacks United States at Pearl Harbor
Germany invades Soviet Union

A.D. 1949
Chinese Communists take over mainland China

A.D. 1945
Atomic bomb used for first time
World War II ends

A.D. 1951
Sputnik launched; first artificial satellite

A.D. 1969
Neil Armstrong first man on the moon

A.D. 1950
Korean War begins

A.D. 1961
Yuri Gagaran first man in space

Renaissance begins in Italy
(approximate date)

Renaissance
A.D. 1400

Gutenberg invents printing
press
A.D. 1450

A.D. 1388
Hundred Years' War begins

A.D. 1403
Chinese Age of Exploration
begins

A.D. 1453
fall of Constantinople to the
Turks

Incas conquered
Reign of "Ivan the Terrible"
begins in Russia
A.D. 1533

Aztecs conquered
A.D. 1519

Columbus reaches the "New
World"
A.D. 1492

A.D. 1543
Copernican Revolution:
Copernicus develops model
of the solar system with sun
at center

A.D. 1526
Babar establishes Mogul Empire
in India

A.D. 1497
Portuguese ships reach India by
sailing around Africa

French Revolution
U.S. Constitution in force;
George Washington elected
first president
A.D. 1789

Japan opened up to the West
A.D. 1854

A.D. 1812
Napoleon invades Russia
War of 1812 between England
and United States

A.D. 1861
U.S. Civil War begins

Adolf Hitler takes power in
Germany
A.D. 1933

Russian Revolution
A.D. 1917

U.S. Civil War ends
A.D. 1865

A.D. 1939
World War II begins with
German invasion of Poland

A.D. 1918
World War I ends

A.D. 1914
First World War begins

War in Viet Nam ends
A.D. 1975

Eastern Europe moves toward
democracy
A.D. 1989

A.D. 1970
First "Earth Day"

A.D. 1985
Mikhail Gorbachev takes over
in Soviet Union; initiates
policies of *glasnost* and
peristroika

A.D. 2000
Popularly considered first year
of new decade, century, and
millennium
World population at 6 billion

THE MARCH OF THE MILLENNIA

A Key to Looking at History

by Isaac Asimov
and Frank White

Walker and Company
New York

First published in the United States of America in 1991
by Walker Publishing Company, Inc.

Published simultaneously in Canada by Thomas Allen & Son
Canada, Limited, Markham, Ontario

Text Design by Georg Brewer

Library of Congress Cataloging-in-Publication Data

Asimov, Isaac, date.
The March of the millennia : a key to looking at history / by
Isaac Asimov and Frank White.
p. cm.
Includes index.
ISBN 0-8027-1122-7
1. Technology and civilization. 2. Civilization—History.
3. Twenty-first century—Forecasts. I. White, Frank, date.
II. Title.
CB478.A77 1991
303.49'09'05—dc20   90-38086
CIP

Printed in the United States of America

2 4 6 8 10 9 7 5 3 1

CONTENTS

INTRODUCTION

The year 2000 is rapidly approaching. In less than a decade it will be here, and people are looking forward to it with a mixture of elation and dread. Will it mark the beginning of a new and happier era or a turning point that will lead the world downward to increased misery? Is it even possible that the year 2000 will bring, as some believe, the end of the world?

We do not know the answers to all of these questions, but this is a good time for asking them by looking ahead and looking back. Those of us living today have an opportunity available to very few human beings—the chance to experience the end and beginning of a year, decade, century, and millennium. It is natural to prepare for such a moment, and perhaps an understanding of the past will help us create a more positive future.

In this book, we will indeed look forward and back, hoping to glean some insights that will help us enter the next millennium with more expectation than fear. We will survey the development of civilization millennium by millennium, beginning in the distant human past of 8000 B.C. and moving forward to the final years before A.D. 2000.

It is not possible, of course, to truly cover all of human history in this way—there is simply too much of it. However, it is possible, perhaps, to find threads of continuity in the roiling changes of the human past. Human population, for example, has continued to grow during this long period and seems likely to continue to do so in the future. What does this mean for the next millennium?

In addition, the human use of energy has been critical to the development of civilization over this period. How will we use energy in the next millennium, especially as our concerns over the state of the environment grow?

The inventive use of technology is another characteristic that constantly appears in any survey of civilization's development over time, and it has become increasingly important in the latter years of this second millennium. What role will technology play in the next millennium?

These and other questions must be considered to prepare ourselves for the next millennium. However, we surely cannot grasp the significance of population, energy, technology, and other subjects today without seeing them in the context of the past. Without knowing where we have come from, we cannot easily detect where we are going.

The next several chapters of this book are, then, a foundation for the final chapter, which directly addresses the issue of what will be the important developments in the next millennium and how we might create a positive future for our descendants.

Before beginning our review, however, we must ask ourselves the most basic question—why do we choose the year 2000 to be a time upon which we pin our hopes and fears?

Perhaps the key is that it is a round number. A year that ends in a 0 sounds significant to us; it is a year that may mark an end or a beginning simply because of its mathematical appearance. A year ending in 00 seems even more significant, and one that ends in 000 seems most significant of all. As it is usually conceived, a year ending in 0 begins a new decade; one ending in 00 a new century; and one ending in 000 a new millennium.

This popular understanding is not exactly correct, of course. If we begin counting with some year that we call 1, then the tenth year is 10, and the years 1 to 10 make up the first decade. It is actually the year 11, therefore, that marks the beginning of the second decade.

By similar reasoning, it is the year 101 that marked the beginning of the second century, and 1001 that inaugurated the beginning of the second millennium. This means that the year 2000 will be the final year of the twentieth century and the second millennium, and it will really be on January 1, 2001 that we begin the twenty-first century and the third millennium.

To persuade humanity to accept that bit of mathematical logic is, however, a hopeless task. On January 1, 2000, we will hear the clamor and noise marking the beginning of the new millennium, and all the pedantic voices saying, "No, no, we must wait another year" will be drowned out and ignored.

We must make the best of it, for even those of us who know better tend to accept the mythic value of 2000 and never think of 2001 as significant, except as a movie title.

Still, the earth is billions of years old and the universe is far older still. Why, then, is the numbering of the years so small? The answer is that humans arbitrarily start counting at a particular *recent* point in history that seems important and unique to us. Naturally, what is important and unique will vary from culture to culture.

The French revolutionaries, for example, were elated over having established, some two centuries ago, a new republic in which they felt that a new era of "liberty, fraternity, and equality" was taking hold. They therefore declared the year 1792 to be the year 1 of the republic. This system continued for about fourteen years, but if it had persisted and been adopted worldwide, what we call the year 2000 would be the year 208 of the republic.

In certain official documents, Americans not only give the year as it is ordinarily accepted but also count the years from the independence of the United States in 1776. The year that we call 2000 would, on that July 4, become the year 224 of American independence.

The Muslim community counts time from the moment when their prophet Muhammad fled from the Arabian city of Mecca to Medina in the year that we call 622. That year became known as the Hegira, (flight) and the event marks their year 1. Also, Muslims use a lunar calendar in which the year is only 354 days long. Thus, the year that we call 2000 will actually be the year A.H. 1421 (the initials standing for "in the year of Hegira") in the Muslim world.

The Greeks of Asia began counting from the year that we call 312 B.C. because that was when their ruler, Seleucus I began his reign. Using this Seleucid era was a popular method for some time, and if it had continued to this day, the year we call 2000 would be 2312 of the Seleucid era.

The Romans had many approaches to this problem, but they eventually settled on counting the years from the founding of Rome, which they placed in the year that we call 753 B.C. They called that year 1 A.U.C., which stands for *Anno Urbis Conditae*, meaning in Latin, "the year of the founding of the city." This method was used in Europe for centuries, and, if it were still used today, the year we call 2000 would be 2752 A.U.C., and the year we call 1247 would have been 2000 A.U.C.

In theory, we could count the years from the beginning of the universe, or the birth of the earth, but that would give us numbers that are impractically large to use in everyday life, such as 10 billion, or 300 million. Moreover, we don't know the exact year that the universe or the earth came into being. Until recently, people hadn't the faintest notion of the true beginnings, and thought that the universe and the earth had been formed in comparatively recent times.

For example, the Jewish rabbis, after studying the Bible thoroughly, decided that the world had begun in the year we call 3760 B.C. Thus the year that we call 2000 would be 5760 of the Jewish Mundane era, mundane deriving from the Latin word for "world." The year 1760 B.C. was, then, the year 2000 of the Jewish Mundane era.

About 1650, an Anglican bishop named James Ussher came up with the year 4004 B.C. for the year of the creation of the world. This date was long accepted as accurate by Protestants, and most Protestant Bibles give it above the account of the Creation at the very beginning of the Bible. Thus, the year we call 2000 would be the year 6004 of the Christian Mundane era.

Our own method of counting time began to be developed around the year 1288 A.U.C., when a scholar named Dionysius Exiguus conducted his own analysis of the Bible. He decided that Jesus Christ had been born 535 years earlier, in 753 A.U.C.

Some 250 years later, Charlemagne, who ruled most of western Europe, decided that it would be much more pious to count the years from the birth of Jesus, rather than from the founding of the city of Rome in the days when it had been heathen. For that reason, 753 A.U.C. became A.D. 1, with A.D. standing for *Anno Domini*, Latin for "the year of our Lord." Earlier dates were then listed as B.C., which stood for "before Christ." With these revisions, Rome was now seen to have been founded in 753 B.C.

The use of this Christian era approach rapidly spread throughout Europe. Then, after 1400, when European ships and guns increasingly dominated the rest of the world, the new system of counting years became global in nature.

Unfortunately, Dionysius Exiguus was wrong in his calculations. The Bible does not give a clear chronology anywhere, and it was therefore easy for him to make a mistake. According to the Bible, Jesus was born when Herod I ruled over Judea. We now know that Herod died in 749 A.U.C. Jesus had to have been born no later than that year, which is 4 B.C. of the Christian era.

If we were *really* counting from the birth of Jesus, the year we call 2000 is really somewhere between 2004 and 2020, and the actual year of A.D. 2000 may already have passed.

It is useless to worry about these anomalies, except insofar as they give us perspective on how relatively arbitrary dates come to have great meaning to us. The year that we call 2000 *is* 2000 to the whole world, and that is the year everyone is anticipating with excitement and trepidation.

As we begin to build our foundation for understanding what the next millennium might bring, the farther back we go in time, the less we really know about the details of people's lives. It was only when human beings had invented the technique of writing that they could record events, and begin what we call history. For that reason, the times before the invention of writing are "prehistoric," and we know what happened only indirectly—by studying the ruins of ancient cities, the remains of pottery and other materials, and examining various other clues.

The earliest millennial period that can be discussed with some degree of confidence is 9000 to 8000 B.C., a time still deep in prehistory. It was in about 8000 B.C., however, that something we call civilization appeared, and that makes for a good beginning.

As long ago as 8000 B.C. might seem, however, it is a short period of time in terms of true Earth history. To create a context for understanding this very early millennium, we must briefly mention some key events that took place even before it began.

CHAPTER ONE

BEFORE CIVILIZATION
THE APPEARANCE OF HUMANS

HUMANS ARE A VERY RECENT ADDITION TO THE UNIVERSE, which came into being billions of years ago. Scientists generally believe that the universe began as an incredibly tiny volume of matter that exploded with unimaginable ferocity at an unimaginably high temperature, and that the aftereffects of that explosion, or Big Bang, are still observable today.

Initially, it was thought that the explosion took place only two billion years ago, but further study pushed that time well back, and current thinking is that the universe was created about fifteen billion years ago.

The universe is made up of many billions of huge star-collections called galaxies, which came into existence not long after the Big Bang. Individual stars have continued to be born and die throughout the lifetime of the universe.

Our sun and its train of planets and other bodies, known as the Solar System, was apparently formed about 4.6 billion years ago. Life on Earth seems to have appeared not long (in cosmic terms) after the planet itself was formed. Beginning in 1954, An American scientist, Elso Sterrenberg Barghoorn, started finding traces of what looked to be the remains of tiny bacteria in ancient rocks. His work suggested that life must have existed on Earth for at least 3.5 billion years.

For some 2,000 million years, life on Earth consisted only of various kinds of bacterial forms. About 1,400 million years ago, however, more complicated types of cells developed. These were eukaryotic cells, and it is these cells that make up all living things that are more complex than bacteria—including ourselves.

Even after these complex cells appeared, life on Earth was primitive, made up of organisms consisting of only one cell (unicellular organisms). Over time, cells began to bind themselves together to form more complex organisms in which various cells specialized and performed different functions. The first of these multicellular organisms may have come into existence about 800 million years ago. All forms of life large enough to be seen without a magnifying glass are multicellular, including human beings. Thus, the multicellular organisms were a successful evolutionary experiment.

The unicellular and early multicellular organisms were soft, made up mostly of water. When they died, they usually disintegrated and left behind very few traces; as a result, we know very little about them today.

Beginning about 600 million years ago, however, organisms started to develop hard parts—shells, for instance, and later, bones and teeth. These remained behind after death when the rest of the animal disintegrated, and over time they were changed chemically into rocky substances called fossils.

From these fossils, scientists began to see that life gradually changed over the millions of years, with some types of organisms dying out or becoming extinct, while others slowly evolved into new forms. Such changes are known as biological evolution, and scientists became curious as to what brought about these developments.

The first scientist to work out a satisfactory theory of evolution was the British biologist, Charles Robert Darwin, who published his views on the subject in 1859. Darwin argued that evolution was driven largely by a process known as natural selection. Species adapted to changes in their environment; new features that contributed to their survival were selected and passed on to the next generation. Less successful individuals often died before they could reproduce, so only the best genes were normally passed on. This idea gave rise to the often-misused phrase, "survival of the fittest," to describe the essence of Darwin's theory.

By 600 million years ago, when fossils first began to appear in quantity, living organisms could already be seen as divided into numerous general categories called phyla (singular, phylum). The phylum to which humans belong is called Chordata, and the earliest chordates first appeared about 550 million years ago.

Even after the earth had completed 90 percent of its present existence, life was still confined to the water, and the land areas of the earth remained sterile. About 450 million years ago, however, plant life began to invade the land, developing stems, roots, and leaves. Spiders and insects followed the plant life as early colonizers of the land.

At that time, the most advanced chordates were the fish. Then, about 370 million years ago, an evolutionary development of great importance took place—certain fish emerged from the sea and developed adaptations that made land-life possible for them.

At first, such land chordates had to return to the water to lay their eggs and bear their young. Then, about 300 million years ago, eggs with shells were developed, allowing the young to be born on land. Reptiles that we now call dinosaurs used this adaptation to evolve and become rulers of the land.

Primitive mammals, the group to which we belong, first appeared about 220 million years ago. For the most part, they were small creatures and continued to survive only by keeping out of the way of the dinosaurs.

Then, about 100 million years ago, the mammals developed another important adaptation—the placenta, which made it possible to keep the young within the mother's body for an extended period of time. The young were born in a relatively advanced form, and this gave mammals an evolutionary advantage.

About 70 million years ago, the first members of a group of mammals called primates made their appearance, and it is to this group that humans belong. Even then, however, the reptiles—especially the dinosaurs—dominated the land. However, a remarkable thing happened. Some 65 million years ago, the dinosaurs simply disappeared. The exact cause of their demise remains unknown, but evidence has been accumulating that a comet collided with the earth during that epoch. Such a collision would set off tidal waves and conflagrations and heave so much dust into the upper atmosphere that the rays of the sun would be blocked for a long time.

Under those circumstances, some forms of life, especially small mammals, would survive, but many others, such as the dinosaurs, would become extinct. Thus, with the large reptiles gone, the mammals evolved rapidly. Some remained small but specialized, developing their brains to a greater extent than any other life-form had done before them. Among the primates, the first monkeys appeared some 40 million years ago, and the first apes about 30 million years ago.

About 5 million years ago, evolution took a new turn, as the first humanlike primates appeared. They were closer to the human beings living today than to any ape, living or extinct. These primates walked erect on two legs, exactly as we do (and as apes do not) and they are called hominids. The earliest of them were called australopithecines, and the first remains of these creatures were studied by the anthropologist Raymond Arthur Dart, beginning in 1924.

For about three million years, the only hominids that existed were different species of australopithecines, found only in eastern and southern Africa. About two million years ago, however, one of the hominid varieties seemed so close to us that it could be placed in the same genus (a group of species) as humans, a genus called *Homo* (Latin for "man"). The new variety was named *Homo habilis* and its remains were first located by British anthropologist Louis S. B. Leakey, in the 1960s.

Homo habilis was the first hominid with the capability of manufacturing stone tools. Using primitive stone axes and knives, they hunted animals and learned how to cut them up for food. Hominids had previously been gatherers of plant food and scavengers of animal food killed by the large carnivores. Now, they could kill and eat their own prey.

About 1.6 million years ago, a new and larger hominid appeared on the scene—*Homo erectus*. This was the first hominid to expand its range beyond Africa, making its way into Asia, probably in pursuit of game herds.

Eventually, they reached all the way to the Pacific and some of the islands off southeastern Asia. The first discoveries of *Homo erectus* were made in Java by a Dutch anthropologist, Eugene Dubois, in 1894. *Homo erectus* turned out to be very successful, and by some 1 million years ago, they were the only hominids left on Earth.

Then, about 600,000 years ago, the earth entered into the first of a series of ice ages. As the overall temperature of the planet cooled, giant sheets of ice moved down from the northern regions farther south. When these glaciers reached their peak, the sea level dropped as much as three hundred feet, exposing land-bridges between nearby areas. This change must have made it possible for *Homo erectus* to wander from Africa into Asia and then on to the Indonesian islands.

The ice ages stimulated adaptation by all life-forms, including hominids. In response to the colder weather that then prevailed, *Homo erectus* wore furs, built weather shelters in the form of tents, lived in caves, and learned to build fires and keep them going. The discovery of fire, a crucial shift in humanity's relationship with energy, took place about 500,000 years ago. The ability to control energy in this way became a dominant theme in the evolution of civilization and humanity's interaction with the environment, and continues to have great importance today.

About 300,000 years ago, the first hominids with brains as large as our own appeared on the world scene. The first trace of these hominids was found in 1856 in the Neander Valley (Neanderthal) in Germany. These hominids were called Neanderthal men.

The skulls of the Neanderthals were distinctly less human than our own, with pronounced eyebrow ridges, large teeth, protruding jaws, a retreating forehead and smoothly receding chin. They were shorter and stockier than we are, and more muscular. Nevertheless, except for the skull, they resemble us so closely that many consider them a variety of our own species: *Homo sapiens* (Latin for "man, the wise").

About 50,000 years ago, human beings like us made their first appearance. By 30,000 years ago, Neanderthal was extinct, and the only species of hominid that had survived 30,000 years of evolution was modern man.

Until this time, hominids had been confined to what is called the World Island—Africa, Asia, and Europe, together with some offshore islands. Some time before 25,000 years ago, however, human beings took advantage of a low sea level during one of the ice ages, advancing from northeastern Asia into North America, and from the Indonesian islands into Australia. In time, human beings penetrated to the farthest reaches of the new lands, down to Tierra del Fuego, off the southern tip of South America; and to Tasmania, off the southeastern tip of Australia.

These early versions of modern humanity were every bit as human as we. They left behind cave paintings as artistic as anything we have done since. Such cave paintings were first discovered in 1879 in a cave in northern Spain.

The paintings were so good that at first people refused to believe that they were really ancient—until other such cave paintings were found. Some of the best of these paintings were found in a cave in the Cro-Magnon area of France, and so these early humans were dubbed Cro-Magnon man.

Precivilized human beings formed societies that were, at first, made up of human beings only. Though there are cases of species that cooperate with other species instinctively (some ants keep aphids for the secretions they produce, for example), humans were the first deliberately to seek out the aid of other animals. We were also the first to set about consciously domesticating other species.

The first such domesticated animals were dogs, which may have begun living with human beings as long as 14,000 years ago.

All dogs, even the most unlikely looking, are descendants of wolves. How they came to be domesticated is unknown, but it began a process that is so common today we take it for granted.

Dogs, being descended from pack animals, would accept a human master as the pack leader. The dog would go hunting with its master, help in tracking and killing the game, and then be satisfied with a minor share of the kill for itself.

Success with one species would probably have led to the domestication of other animals. By 12,000 years ago, for example, goats may have been domesticated in the Middle East. The goats would be cared for, fed, and encouraged to reproduce. They could supply milk, butter, and cheese, and, by judicious culling, they could be a meat supply as well.

Whereas dogs ate food that would otherwise fill human stomachs, goats ate grass and other substances that humans found inedible, so that the human food supply was increased at no cost.

Other animals also were eventually domesticated—cattle, sheep, camels, chickens, and geese. The food supply of human beings who possessed herds and flocks became far more secure in this way. As a result, there was less need to hunt and kill on a hit-or-miss basis. Domestication promised a perpetual food supply, barring disease, failure of rain, and predators, and human beings began to live more easily.

It is important to see, then, that human civilization is a relatively recent invention. Even as we look at it developing over 11,000 years, this is a short period of time compared to the preparatory stages that preceded its emergence. It may also be a short period of time in terms of its future development.

In any event, this phase brings us to the beginning of civilization, which we can place at 8000 B.C. With that we begin to follow the millennia.

CHAPTER TWO

THE PREHISTORIC MILLENNIA

(8000–4000 B.C.)

The Agricultural Transformation

BY 8000 B.C., SOME TEN THOUSAND YEARS AGO, THE LAST period of glaciation that Earth has so far experienced was drawing to its close. The glaciers had receded, and Earth's climate was beginning to resemble what it is today.

The disappearance of the glaciers brought about great changes. The storm belts and the rain retreated northward with the glaciers. Northern Africa, for example, ceased to be lush grassland as it dried out and formed the Sahara Desert.

The land-bridges joining Asia with North America in the north, and with Australia in the south, were flooded as the sea level rose again. The people who occupied the Americas and Australia were separated from the main population on the World Island for thousands of years.

The shores of the Arctic Ocean were gradually being cleared of a permanent ice cover, and the people we now know as Inuits (Eskimos), Lapps, and Siberians began drifting northward.

The Middle East, the land that borders the eastern Mediterranean Sea, the Caspian Sea, and the Persian Gulf was, of all the world's regions, the most advanced technologically.

The Middle Eastern population still made their tools out of stone, so that they lived in the Stone Age, as did all human beings at this time. The Middle Easterners, however, were also learning to make the stone tools more sophisticated so that they lived in what we now call the New Stone Age, or (in Latin) the Neolithic period. It was the Middle Eastern peoples who first domesticated animals and made other advances that increased the security of life and led to a regional increase in population. This is sometimes called the Neolithic revolution, and is said to have initiated the first population explosion.

This critical relationship between technology development, increased security, and population growth is another theme that will continue to echo throughout future millennia.

World population at 4 million

The human population of the world may have been 4 million in 8000 B.C., and of these perhaps 500,000, or one-eighth, of the total may have lived in the Middle East. We do not know why the people of the Middle East made these advances, rather than people living elsewhere. It may have been partly the result of accident—brought about, for instance, by the fact that animals suited for domestication just happened to live in the region. However, we will see that the leadership by a particular region of the world in developing new civilizations continually shifts over the millennia, with no particular area holding on to supremacy for very long.

In any event, the greater density of population in the Middle East brought about by the Neolithic revolution encouraged still greater advances. After all, the more people there are at any given time, the greater the chance that one of them might have a brilliant idea. Also, the more people there are, the more complex the society, and the greater the pressure to think of solutions to social problems.

Of course, this does not mean that increasing the population is always beneficial. The advantages are apparent only if there is room to absorb the increase. If the population increases beyond the space available or food supply to support it, the disadvantages rapidly outweigh the advantages.

With the retreat of the glaciers and the changing of the climate, large stands of wild grain grew over the Middle East, leading to another change, perhaps the most important since the development of the use of fire. Human beings now began to domesticate plants.

Somewhere about 8000 B.C., in what is now northern Iraq, people learned how to cultivate such grains as wheat and barley. They planted seeds deliberately, pulled up competing plants (weeds), frightened off the animals who wanted to eat the grain, and did their best to see that water was supplied when the plants needed it. Finally, when the grain was ripe, they harvested it, saved an ample seed supply for future planting, and roasted what was left over for food.

They also learned to grind the grain into a flour that kept without spoiling for a long time when the outer layer of the ears of grain was removed. The flour could then be baked into a nourishing, long-lasting, hard, flat bread.

Such grain domestication marked the beginning of *agriculture*   **Agriculture invented** (Latin for "field cultivation"). The invention of agriculture, like that of herding, supplied more food for the population engaged in it. Agriculture, however, was far superior to herding in this respect: animals convert plant life into meat, but in doing so, they preserve only a small amount of the total energy available in plants. If human beings feed on plants directly, much more food energy is available to them than if they feed on animals that have eaten plants. A given plot of land can support far more human beings if it is devoted to agriculture than if it is devoted to herding.

The result of the agricultural transformation was that population increased markedly wherever it was practiced. There were disadvantages, of course. Farming was tedious and backbreaking work. It offered none of the glamor and excitement of hunting or the ease and relaxation of herding. Farmers probably looked back on the tales of hunting done by their ancestors, and viewed the hunting/herding practices of their nonagricultural neighbors with a certain envy. They may have viewed agriculture as a kind of slavery foisted upon them, which even the use of animal labor couldn't fully mitigate.

It is not surprising, then, that so many agricultural communities imagined a "golden age" in which human beings hunted and gathered in freedom and comparative idleness. They would have wondered what had happened to evict them and force them to earn their bread by the sweat of their brow. The Hebrew tale of Eden and of the sin that caused God to curse humanity with agriculture is perhaps the best known of these stories.

Nevertheless, no matter how much people might dislike farming and long for a happier, freer day, there was no way that agriculture could be abandoned once it had been adopted. The population of an agricultural region quickly reached a peak that could not be supported by any other methods. To abandon argiculture and try to feed the population by herding and hunting meant mass starvation. Agriculture, with all its faults, was the only reasonable way of seeing to it that large populations had full stomachs.

Indeed, the advantages of agriculture in that respect were so obvious that it spread to all suitable regions, and is now a worldwide phenomenon. This spreading process took place at the expense of herding and hunting cultures (the latter were slowly wiped out). Thus, the Bible tells how, of Adam and Eve's first two sons, Cain (the farmer) slew Abel (the herdsman).

Agriculture brought on another major change in how people lived. Hominids had been wandering people, seeking out plants or following game over wide ranges. Even when herding began, the herdsmen still had to wander about to find good pasture for their animals. They were *nomads*, from a Greek word meaning "pasture."

Hunters and herdsmen could not remain in one place even if they wanted to do so, because the animal life in a particular region was soon killed or scared off, and all the plant life was consumed. There had to be an endless search for new ground, therefore, with a return to old ground only after enough time had been given for it to recover.

Nomads could not have possessions that were not portable, nothing that could not be abandoned as needed, nothing that would correspond to "home," except for temporary sites. Some

such sites, to be sure, might have gained a kind of semiperman-
ence if they were well situated. It would be in those places where
agriculture would have been developed, for the growing of plants
would be useless if nomads did not remain in place for a least a
growing season.

Once agriculture had been established, however, there was no
longer any question of temporary, or even semipermanent. Plots
of land that had been cleared of weeds, that had been planted,
and that had to be tended *could not be moved*. Because plots of land
were immovable, farmers, unlike preceding generations, had to
adopt a settled life. They had to stay in one place, and the notion
of "property" became far more important than it had been before.

Agriculture stimulated another change, as well. In the days of
wandering, one roving band might meet another, resulting in a
quarrel as to which had the right to exploit the area. The matter
might degenerate into a mutual display of force, but this was
rarely deadly, because it would quickly become apparent which
band was the stronger. The weaker group, foreseeing inevitable
defeat, would retreat, abandon the area, and search for another.
There was rarely anything in any one area worth the risk of their
lives.

When farming began, the situation was different. Farmers
became a natural object of attack, for they had usually put away
stores of grain to feed themselves over the winter, and nomads
might well view the stores with greedy eyes. They might also see
no reason why they should not appropriate it if they could. In
such a case, the farmers did not have the option of retreating—
defending their immovable farms meant that they had to fight.
They had no choice but to risk defeat, since giving up their land
meant that they would die of starvation or be forced to sell
themselves into slavery in return for food.

Thus, the advent of agriculture meant that there could be
greater populations living a life that was somewhat more secure
than the hunter/herder cultures could manage. However, it also
inevitably meant the invention of organized warfare, an institution
that has survived through the millennia to the present day.

If the farmers had to fight, it was only prudent to take measures

Organized warfare
begins

that would make defeat less likely. It would have been very risky to remain scattered among their farms, where they could easily be destroyed, one family at a time.

Instead, the natural strategy was to collect together, setting up their homes in a tightly packed fashion, from which they could move outward to their farms by day, returning at night. They could retreat to these homes at the first sign of a threatened attack and, fighting together, hold off the enemy.

The chances of defeating the enemy were also increased if they set their homes on an elevation so that the attackers would have to hurl their missiles upward, while the defenders threw theirs downward. The homes would also ideally include a spring that would serve as a dependable water supply and places where food could be stored and protected. Of course, it would help if a wall were built around the homes.

Cities appear   In short, once agriculture was instituted, the city was sure to follow. The city meant less individual space for people, reduced freedom of movement, more complicated arrangements for bringing in food, disposal of wastes, and providing for the common defense—but it also promised much greater security. In most cases, people were willing to trade some of their freedom for security.

The city, plus the surrounding farms that belonged to the city dwellers, made up a community that came to be called a city-state.

Once a city-state had become a going proposition, and a reasonable level of security was established, the community could grow more food than it consumed. It therefore became possible for some people *not* to be farmers, and to do other kinds of useful work. Some might be artisans, specializing in the manufacture of tools and ornaments; others might be soldiers, merchants, or government officials. They all essentially did their work in return for food, while farmers paid with food for the services of these nonfarmers. In this way, a differentiated society, of the type that we still have today, first came into being.

Almost everyone benefited from these arrangements, and the standard of living advanced. Thus, the invention of agriculture initiated an ongoing drive toward urbanization, by 8000 B.C., a trend continuing today at breakneck speed all over the world.

The appearance of the city marked the true beginnings of civilization as we know it. Since this very early millennium, great cities have always been the heart of great civilizations. In Latin, the word for city-dweller is *civis*, and the adjective derived from it is *civillis*. Civilization is, quite simply, the kind of society that is marked by agriculture and cities.

Beginning of civilization

Civilization did not spread everywhere and to everyone at once. Rather, it began in isolated spots in the Middle East and was barely a factor in 8000 B.C. In northern Iraq, there are the remains of a very ancient city, founded perhaps as early as 8000 B.C., at a site called Jarmo. It is a low mound into which the American archeologist, Robert J. Braidwood, began to dig in 1948. He found the remains of foundations of houses built of thin walls of packed mud and divided into small rooms. Jarmo may have housed a population from one hundred to three hundred people.

Another city that may date back to the earliest days of agriculture is Jericho, near the Jordan River. Jericho is famous as the city whose walls fell before the trumpets of the nomadic Israelites, led by Moses' successor, Joshua.

Thus, the period from 9000 to 8000 B.C. is characterized by a fundamental change in how human beings lived, brought about as the transition from a nomadic to a settled lifestyle. This shift was made possible by the invention of something that we now take for granted—agriculture. Without it the innovations of the succeeding millennia could not have occurred.

7000 B.C.

ORIGINALLY, AGRICULTURE WAS PRACTICED IN REGIONS where the rains were reliable—at the base of mountains for example. There, the prevailing winds were forced upward and cooled, so that their water vapor content was frequently precipitated out.

Extending the Human Reach

On the whole, though, the Middle East continued to grow more arid after the Ice Age came to an end, and the rains became less reliable. The farming areas, therefore, shifted in the direction of large, flowing rivers. The river served as a dependable and perpetual fresh water supply, and farmers no longer had to depend on the fickle rainfall.

The nearest large river to the places in northern Iraq where early agriculture was practiced, was the Euphrates River, and its twin, the Tigris. The nearest large river to Palestine, where agriculture also had a foothold, was the Nile River.

By 7000 B.C., agriculture was being established along the course of these three rivers. Now, for the first time, patches of civilization began to appear in the world. The first was in the Tigris-Euphrates Valley, which was, in ancient times, called Babylonia, after a large and famous city in the region. The second was in the Nile Valley and was known to the later Greeks, and to us, as Egypt.

Irrigation begins

Using rivers for moisture is an improvement over depending on rain, but there is a catch. When it rains, water falls all over the field in which crops are growing. The farmer doesn't have to do anything to get the water to where it is needed. If the farmer depends on the river, however, he can wait indefinitely, as the water is not likely to come to the crops of its own accord, except when it floods, which has disastrous side effects.

The inventive farmers of the time solved that problem by digging irrigation ditches into which the river water could flow to the crops. The farmer had to work to keep the ditches dredged so that they didn't silt up and lose their functionality. He also had to build levees to hold the river back when the floods did come. Once again farmers had to take on additional labor as a payment for increased security. In addition, irrigating the land was clearly a community endeavor, and it had to be carefully organized and supervised. Thus, the value of the city as a means of organizing human activities grew as irrigation became more widespread.

The river cities were only beginning to appear in 7000 B.C., and the older cities still held pride of place at that time. Jericho, in particular, was probably the largest city in the world during this era. It extended over an area of about ten acres and boasted a population of some 2,500.

Embryonic as these beginnings were, the outlines of civilization's future evolution became clear during this period. Civilization demanded the human management of natural processes, rather than dependence on nature's own cycles, for example. This, in turn, required new forms of human organization. Irrigation, which is still widely practiced today, allowed humans to establish settlements in regions previously barred to them.

Over time, the invention of other technologies would continue to extend the human reach.

6000 B.C.

The Proliferation of Technology

B Y 6000 B.C., THE PRACTICE OF AGRICULTURE HAD SPREAD west and north into Asia Minor and southeastern Europe. As agriculture progressed, it encouraged innovation and invention. Rice, for example, began to be cultivated in southeastern Asia and is one of the main food sources of that region today.

New cities began to overtake and surpass the old. There was a city at a site known to us as Catalhuyuk, in south-central Asia Minor, which reached its peak in 6000 B.C. and was probably the largest city in the world at that time. The site was excavated in the early 1960s by the British archeologist, James Mellaart, and found to cover thirty-two acres.

Remains found at Catalhuyuk included another important human invention of the prehistoric period—pottery. Pottery is an outstanding type of relic at these ancient sites of civilization, partly because pottery was useful and easy to make, so that it was produced in large quantities. In addition, unlike other objects that might have been equally important, pottery survives over long periods of time. Like the creatures whose hard shells survived as fossils when their softer predecessors have disappeared, pottery persists and provides us with a historical record of the times before writing was invented.

Pottery developed

Pottery arose out of the very human need to carry things. The natural carryalls are the hands and the arms, but both are limited in size. Objects can be carried in hides, but these are inconvenient, stiff, and heavy.

Gourds might work, but they could only be used when they could be found growing naturally. Eventually, people learned to weave twigs or reeds into baskets that were light and could be made in any size or shape. Baskets, however, would only be useful in carrying solid, dry objects made of particles larger than the interstices of the weave. Baskets could not be used to carry flour or olive oil, or, most important, water.

It was possible to daub baskets with moist clay, which, upon drying, would cake the holes. Then, if the basket was placed in the sunlight and allowed to heat there, the mud would harden further and the basket would become more servicable. However, the dried mud would fall away after a time.

It must have occurred to someone that the basket wasn't needed at all. Why not simply begin with clay, mold a container out of it, and let it dry in the sun? You would then have a pot made of crude earthenware. Unfortunately, the sun's heat was not enough to make the pot hard and durable; something more was needed.

Clay could be subjected to a stronger heat by being placed directly in a fire. Fired earthenware became hard pottery, and its production represents the first use of fire for something other than light, heat, and cooking.

By 6000 B.C., pottery had become a well-established product. Pottery made it possible not only to carry liquids but also to cook meat in boiling water. In this way, the human diet was expanded, as stews and casseroles came into being.

Someone else noticed that the idea behind the weaving of twigs into baskets was applicable to fibers that were much thinner, provided that they were strong enough. Flax produces a fiber suitable for the purpose, and flax was being cultivated well before 6000 B.C. It may have been the first plant cultivated for a purpose other than food.

Flax fibers can be woven together to form a long thread, which we call linen. The importance of a linen thread as an example of something long and straight can be surmised from the fact that the word "line" comes from linen.

Textiles developed   By now, farming along riverbanks was becoming much more important, and rivers became essential to human life in other ways, as well. The river was a source of food, for example, and the first use of linen may well have been to form interwoven nets for fishing. Eventually, people made very fine nets, which we now call cloth or *textiles* (from a Latin word for "weaving"). The creation of cloth from linen, and eventually from other plant and animal fibers such as cotton or wool, revolutionized clothing.

Textiles are light materials. They are flexible, porous, and can be easily cleaned. As a result, they have remained the preferred material for clothing ever since.

A river also offers a means of transportation. Its level surface is much easier to negotiate than the rough unevenness of land, but a means of moving along a river's surface without sinking and drowning, must be found. Humans must have observed very early in their history that wood floats, and by 6000 B.C., people had learned to lash logs together to form rafts.

Rafts would keep passengers safely on the surface of quiet bodies of water and enable them to fish more efficiently than from the shore. By paddling (with their hands if nothing else), they could even cross small bodies of water.

Once again, the mastery of water extended the human reach. All of a sudden, travel time was shortened, and the work necessary to go from one place to another was drastically reduced. Communities might be separated by many miles but still remain in fairly continual communication through river transportation, and new areas could be explored far more easily.

At the same time, the domestication of animals continued apace, further contributing to the stability and security of human life. The wild ox was tamed and became the ancestor of modern cattle, a particularly important source of meat, dairy products, and leather. Herding and farming were now joined together as a means of sustaining human communities.

As we move toward 5000 B.C., it is possible to see the foundations of modern society being laid, brick by brick, as human inventiveness slowly provides our ancestors with advantages over the natural environment and its other inhabitants.

5000 B.C.

AS 5000 B.C. DAWNED, CIVILIZATION HAD EXISTED IN THE Tigris-Euphrates Valley for some three thousand years. Civilization was also spreading to other areas of the world, and the use of technologies to enhance the quality of life was accelerating.

The Dominance of the City-State

Sumerians enter
Tigris-Euphrates
Valley

At this time, a new group of people, the Sumerians, entered the Tigris-Euphrates Valley. We do not know the origins of the Sumerians, partly because their language is not related to any other, preventing us from tracing relationships.

The Sumerians turned out to be a remarkable people. They learned what was being done by their predecessors in the valley, and then carried matters much farther. They were the first group

City-states dominant
political form

to develop what we call a high civilization.

By 5000 B.C., the Sumerians had established working city-states along the lower course of the Euphrates River and were exploiting irrigation to the fullest possible extent. Theirs were the largest and most important cities in the world in 5000 B.C.

They also improved river transportation. For example, it was easy to let a raft drift downstream in the direction of the river current, but it was hard to move against the current. The Sumerians appear to have been the first to use sails of strong textile material to overcome this problem. The sail trapped the wind, and this drove the ships in the wind's direction, even against the river current.

The downstream portion of the Tigris-Euphrates is usually referred to as Sumeria during this period, though the Bible calls it Shinar. The tale of the Tower of Babel is located there, and many people think that the legendary Garden of Eden was situated there as well.

Priest-kings become
city-state rulers

The Sumerians also developed a major political concept. As the city-states grew in importance, the rulers felt that they needed to gain unquestioned authority if they were to organize society effectively. The logical way was to associate the ruler with the divine in some way. He therefore became a priest-king, capable of interceding with the gods on behalf of his people, making sure that all the affairs of the city would remain successful and prosperous.

A priestly hierarchy was eventually established to serve as the bureaucracy of the city-state. The Sumerians built temples as homes for the gods and priests, as repositories of government records and storehouses for grain. Religion became institutionalized and functioned as a major pillar of support for the state, which has continued to be one of its primary functions ever since.

During this period, the same advances in river agriculture and associated religious institutions also began to develop along the Nile River. Egypt and Sumeria were close enough to each other so that travelers from one might reach the other, trade could take place between them, and institutions could be copied. Undoubtedly, each region served the other as a source of ideas and innovations.

Meanwhile, advances continued in other parts of the world, as well. For example, in the Andean region of northern South America, the llama and alpaca (small South American relatives of the camel of Asia and Africa) were domesticated. In Mexico, the farmers learned to grow cotton and avocadoes, while dates were now being grown in south Asia. In the steppes north of the Black Sea, the horse was domesticated, promising changes in land transportation that rivaled developments along the rivers.

In this millennium, the city-state evolved and matured as an effective form of organization, headed by the divine ruler, and used new techniques to manage human activities around the globe.

World population at 5 million

4000 B.C.

From Stone to Metal

J AMES USSHER HAD CALCULATED THAT THE EARTH AND THE universe were created just a few years before 4000 B.C. However, recent research shows that he set a ludicrously late date for the Creation. By that time, civilization, itself a very late phenomenon in the history of Earth, was already four thousand years old.

The Sumerian city of Ur was founded about 4000 B.C. at the mouth of the Euphrates River. In those days, the Euphrates and the Tigris entered the Persian Gulf separately. In the 6,000 years since then, however, silt has filled in the gulf for about 150 miles so that the remains of Ur are now that far from the sea. Across those 150 miles of silt, the Tigris and Euphrates flowed together, and now the combined river flows some 50 miles into the retreated coastline of the gulf.

City of Ur founded

For quite a long time, Ur was the most important city in the world, and perhaps the largest in the world. Our knowledge of Ur in particular, and of Sumeria in general, began to develop in the 1920s, thanks to the work of the British archeologist, Charles Leonard Woolley (1880–1960).

By this time, the people of the Middle East had learned about the fermentation of grape juice and soaked barley, resulting in wine and beer. These drinks were popular, as they are today, because they induced intoxication, which felt good in moderation.

Such beverages were important in another way, although the early drinkers could scarcely be aware of it. Alcohol tends to kill microorganisms, so that drinking wine and beer proved to be safer than drinking water that might be contaminated with human and animal wastes.

It was not, however, for the invention of alcoholic beverages that this millennium should be remembered. It is more notable because it witnessed a fundamental shift in the technology of tool making. Until now, over a period of two million years, human beings and their hominid predecessors had used stone and stone-like substances such as pottery as the chief material for tools. The entire period of hominid history before 4000 B.C. is often called the Stone Age. (This phrase was first used by the Roman poet, Titus Lucretius Carus [95–55 B.C.] about 60 B.C., and then reintroduced in 1834 by the Danish archeologist, Christian Jurgenson Thomsen [1788–1865].)

Stone tools sufficed for many purposes but they had their drawbacks. We can imagine that people in those times would welcome opportunities to improve on what they had, and occasionally they did find pebbles that were not like other stones. These unusual pebbles were shinier and heavier than ordinary rocks. What's more, if they were struck with a stone hammer, they did not split or shatter as ordinary pebbles did, but underwent a simple distortion of shape—they were malleable.

These unusual substances were metals. We now know about dozens of different metals, but most of them remain in combination with nonmetallic substances and form the ordinary rocks and pebbles all around us. Only those metals that tend not to combine with other substances are likely to be found free. The three inert metals most likely to be found in free form—copper, silver, and gold—are rare. Their rarity is shown by the fact that the very word *metal* is derived from a Greek term meaning "to search for."

Metal nuggets were at first used almost exclusively for ornaments, after being pounded into attractive shapes. It was only when people discovered that metals could be obtained from special rocks called ores that they became common enough to be used for other purposes.

Copper is much more common than silver and gold, and it exists in certain ores to a far greater extent then silver and gold do. The most common copper ore is a kind of copper carbonate, which is blue. It contains, in addition to copper, carbon (best known to us in the form of coal) and oxygen.

The discovery of metal ores probably came about by accident. A wood fire might have been built on a bed of rock that happened to contain copper ore. Under the heat of the fire, the carbon in the wood and in the ore would combine with the oxygen in the ore and in the atmosphere to form the gas known as carbon dioxide, which would then escape. Metallic copper would have been left behind.

Eventually, some observant person might have noticed the reddish globules of copper among the ashes of the fire, globules that had not been there before. She, or someone else, might have guessed at the circumstances that had produced them. Once the process was understood, people would search for the ores and deliberately treat them so as to obtain the metal.

Here, then, was another critically important use of fire. By **Metallurgy invented** 4000 B.C., metallurgy—obtaining of metals from their ores—had come into existence, heralding the beginning of the end of the Stone Age.

As with all such advances, knowledge of the new technique diffused outward from its point of origin (probably somewhere in the Middle East). In this case, diffusion stopped at the edge of the ocean, and metallurgy never reached the Americas or Australia, nor did the people of those continents discover the technique on their own.

Meanwhile, civilization itself continued to spread outward. A third river valley had begun to develop into a home for city-states by 4000 B.C.—the Indus River, which flows through what we now call Pakistan. In 1921 and 1922, remains of an early civilization were found along that river by the British archeologist, John Humbert Marshall (1876–1958).

World population at 7 million

By 4000 B.C., then, the human impact on Earth had become increasingly noticeable and important. In only four millennia, humans had spread their civilizations from a tenuous beginning to become a tenacious presence on planet Earth.

CHAPTER THREE

HISTORY BEGINS

(3000–1000 B.C.)

(*Author's Note:* Italicized dates in parentheses are periods of rulers' reigns; other dates in parentheses indicate rulers' lifespans.)

3000 B.C.

The Writing Revolution

AS WE MOVE FROM 4000 B.C. TO 3000 B.C., SEVERAL CRITIcal changes take place around the world. New discoveries in metallurgy usher in the Bronze Age, and the wheel is widely used for the first time. As important as these innovations might have been, however, it is the invention of writing that holds our attention and transforms our knowledge of the past.

Let's look first at the development of bronze as a widely used metal. The process begins with copper. When copper was obtained from ore, it meant that there was a much greater supply of the metal for ornamental use, but at first it was not very practical as a material for tool making.

If the sharp edge of a piece of rock was blunted, that edge had to be restored by laborious chipping, or the rock had to be discarded altogether. If a sharp-edged piece of copper was blunted, however, it could simply be beaten sharp again. The difficulty was that while stone was hard and might survive for a long time without losing its edge, copper was much softer and every minor use bent and blunted it.

Over time, people discovered that not all copper was the same, and this led to another innovation. Copper obtained from some ores turned out to be harder than from others. The reason is that copper ore is not necessarily pure; it might be mixed with other ores and a metallic substance might be obtained that is a mixture, or alloy, of copper and another metal.

Eventually, it was discovered that a judicious mixture of copper and tin ore yielded an alloy called bronze (possibly from a Persian word for copper). Bronze was hard enough to compete with rock, it could also hold an edge better and be beaten back into shape if necessary.

Bronze Age begins   By 3000 B.C., the Sumerians and neighboring peoples were using bronze so extensively that western Asia was entering what is now called the Bronze Age.

The clever Sumerians also introduced another major advance without which civilization could not have proceeded much further—the wheel. Its first use may have been as the potter's wheel. In making pottery, clay was first molded into shape by hand, with the result that the pot was rarely smooth or symmetrical but more likely to be knobby and wobbly.

If, however, a blob of clay was placed on a flat, circular rock that pivoted on a projection beneath, the rock could be made to turn rapidly. A touch of the hand on the spinning clay produced a symmetrical cylinder that could be given interesting shapes by changing the hand pressure at different heights. Using a potter's wheel produced beautiful pottery in far less time than anything made by hand.

Wheels first used for transportation   Once wheels became common, people thought of turning them vertical and placing them on the four ends of a cart. The two front wheels and the two rear wheels could each be connected by an axle suspended from leather straps. The cart then rolled while the wheels moved along with it. This method made it far easier to transport materials overland than by dragging them over rough, uneven ground, or using rollers that remained behind as the vehicle moved, and had to be continually moved themselves.

Naturally, for wheels to work well they needed to move over relatively smooth ground. For that purpose, lanes were freed of vegetation and rocks. Carts, in other words, made a road network necessary, and by 3000 B.C., roads and wheeled carts were common in western Asia.

It was still easier to travel by water, but rivers did not always go where you wanted to go, and the current might be in the wrong direction, or the wind might not be blowing. By 3000 B.C., however, the Sumerians were using oars to drive a boat against the current, even in the absence of a wind blowing in the right direction.

The Sumerians also developed the first simple plows that could be dragged along by donkeys or oxen to scrape up the soil, loosening and aerating it. Seeds scattered through the loose soil then grew more easily and rapidly than if they were merely dropped into a hole that had been punched into hard soil.

The Sumerians had made many important contributions to the world up until this time. However, they surpassed themselves with their most important invention just before 3000 B.C.

In Sumeria, which was the most advanced civilization in the world at this time, life was more complex than elsewhere. People had to keep track of the grain they produced, how much they traded, what other products they manufactured, and the contributions they made to the common fund as taxes.

People found that it was more and more difficult to keep it all in mind, and they looked for a way to keep score. Almost anyone can think of making some sort of mark to stand for each basket of fruit, then eventually counting the marks to know how many baskets had been delivered.

The Sumerians began making such marks, according to an increasingly elaborate system. They divided number marks into different groups; some meant individual items, some meant groups of twelve or sixty. To this day, we still have twelve units to the dozen and sixty minutes to the hour.

They also made special marks that meant "fruit," "grain," "man," and so on. By 3000 B.C., the Sumerians had developed something really special—a system of writing that could communicate anything they wanted to say. It was the first such system of writing in the world.

Writing invented by Sumerians

The Sumerians made the marks of their writing by punching a stylus at an angle into soft clay, and then baking the clay to make the writing permanent. This made wedge-shaped marks, and it was later called *cuneiform* from Greek words meaning "wedge-shaped."

The marks originated as crude pictures of whatever was being talked about, but as time went on, the symbols became simpler and more stylized, losing their pictorial representations. Nevertheless, each symbol stood for a word, more or less, so that there were always hundreds and even thousands of different symbols that someone had to memorize if he or she wanted to read and write.

The complexity of the system meant that literates were always a small minority of the population, and a small but highly valued class of people arose. These were the scribes, who undertook to read and write for the population as a whole.

Writing made an enormous difference in the evolution of human society. Thoughts and records remained much more permanent when written than when spoken. If it is carefully reproduced, writing persists indefinitely. This means that each generation could learn more precisely and quickly the accumulated experience and wisdom of previous generations. The rate of social advancement quickened as a result.

Furthermore, the records kept in writing give us a reasonably exact version of events that took place, complete with names, places, and details. A society that possesses writing is therefore historic, because it records its history (one that does not is prehistoric). In other words, human history truly begins with Sumeria not long before 3000 B.C. Thus, the first five thousand years of civilization were prehistoric and only the last five thousand have been historic.

The Sumerians benefited from their unique position near the Tigris and Euphrates, and their rivals in Egypt were equally fortunate because of the presence of the Nile. Not only was the river a source of water for a land that had grown rainless after the end of the ice ages, but it flooded annually and fertilized the land in a kind of automatic irrigation.

In addition, the current of the Nile was gentle and without storms, so that it was easy to float on it safely. What's more, the river flows almost due north, while the wind almost always blows due south. Therefore, a boat can be carried smoothly downriver (northward) by the current, and returned upriver (southward) by using sails.

Egypt lacked forests, but it had luxuriant stands of reeds (called papyrus) along the river. The reeds could be bundled together to build a boat (when Moses was set afloat in the Nile River, according to the biblical account, he was placed in a little boat, or ark, made of bulrushes, or papyrus).

This particularly easy form of communication brought the various city-states along the Nile into a kind of sympathetic cooperation. They possessed a common language, common culture, and a common worldview. The ease of trade enriched them all, and the region had long periods of peace such as no other region ever experienced.

The city-states of the Nile delta, a triangular section in the north, made up Lower Egypt (because it was downriver) while the city-states of the narrow valley south of the delta were called Upper Egypt.

A union of city-states is a useful mechanism—all the city-states can combine to deal with common problems. For example, it makes more sense to have all of them take care of irrigation problems under unified direction than to have them pulling at cross-purposes. It is better for all if each city-state produces something it is good at producing, and trades the excess for something it does not produce well. It is even better if the trade is regulated by some authority representing all of them.

There is always a unifying tendency that is usually counterbalanced by a disintegrating tendency, since each city-state is bound to feel superior to the others, or resentment over some real or fancied favored treatment others receive. Where the cultures of the various city-states are similar, the unifying tendency may well be stronger than the disintegrating one, and a union may be carried out by a vigorous and capable ruler of one of the city-states.

The ruler who brought this about in Egypt, in about 3000 B.C., was Narmer (the Greeks called him Menes), the first nonlegendary person known by name in history. As ruler of all of Egypt, he established his capital at Memphis, a city built on the border between Lower Egypt and Upper Egypt so that neither region would appear to be dominating the other.

Narmer began Egypt's First Dynasty, a dynasty being a line of rulers from a single family. An Egyptian priest, Manetho, wrote a history of Egypt about 250 B.C., dividing Egyptian rulers into a series of thirty dynasties, and we still follow his system today.

We know about Narmer because during his time or soon after, Egypt learned the technique of writing from the Sumerians. They used their own system, writing with brushes on flattened sheets of papyrus pith and using graceful symbols for various words. These are called *hieroglyphics*, which is Greek for "sacred carvings," the best examples of which are carved in stone in the Egyptian temples.

By 3000 B.C., then, two regions on Earth had entered into historic time: Sumeria and Egypt.

Egypt united into first nation-state

During this time, the fledgling civilizations began to take another major step in the evolution of political forms. When a number of city-states, of similar language and culture, come under the sway of a single ruler, they form a nation-state, or simply a nation. Egypt was the first nation in history, and it is still a nation today, five thousand years later. Egypt holds the undisputed record for national longevity.

Elsewhere, civilization continued to spread, even though writing had not come into use outside of Egypt and Sumeria. To the west of Sumeria lay Elam, with its capital at Susa, just beginning to absorb Sumerian civilization. Farther east, the city-states along the Indus River were developing their political and social cultures, as well.

By 3000 B.C., city-states had also begun to appear along the eastern shores of the Mediterranean, forming a region called Canaan in the Bible and Phoenicia to the Greeks. (It was here, in Canaan, that Jericho had existed for thousands of years.) The Canaanites/Phoenicians had grown strong as merchant middlemen, carrying the rich trade that flowed between Egypt and Sumeria.

In Asia Minor, where Catalhuyuk had once been the largest city in the world, there were other city-states, though these had been outstripped by Sumeria and Egypt. In the northwest of Asia Minor, there were the beginnings of a city that would initially achieve great fame under the name of Troy.

At this time, too, civilization was moving toward Europe; by 3000 B.C., city-states had begun to appear on the island of Crete.

Northern China also fostered the development of new city-states, along the Hwang-ho River (long known in western geographies as the Yellow River). Whereas Sumeria and Egypt formed the nucleus from which civilization spread through all of western Asia and the Mediterranean area, China now formed a second, independent nucleus that served to spread civilization throughout eastern and southeastern Asia.

Until now, the population of the planet had been growing slowly. From about 4 million at the dawn of civilization in 8000 B.C., it had reached only 5 million by 5000 B.C. and about 7 million by 4000 B.C. Then, in the millennium between 4000 B.C. and 3000 B.C., thanks largely to Sumerian inventions such as metallurgy, wheeled transport, oars, and plows, the population spurted upward. It doubled from 7 million to 14 million and almost all of the increase took place in the Middle East.

World population at 14 million

The foundation had now been laid for a burst of new development in the succeeding millennium.

2000 B.C.

DURING THE PERIOD FROM 3000 TO 2000 B.C., THE HUMAN presence on Earth took on a new appearance. Rather than a few scattered pockets sprouting up here and there, many centers of human civilization began to appear, radiating outward and interacting with one another at their peripheries. Some of the older centers prospered, while others fell by the wayside, and new, more vigorous societies rose to take their place.

Many Centers of Civilization

Egypt became the leading region of the world in the centuries that followed its achieving nationhood. When it first became a nation, there may have been 1 million people living along the banks of the Nile. By 2000 B.C., that figure may have risen to 2.5 million.

The increase in population came about because, as a nation, the Egyptians learned to exploit the annual flooding of the Nile and build up a huge surplus of food. This surplus could in turn be traded with other nations at a premium when those countries suffered bad harvests. (The story of Jacob and his sons in the second half of the biblical book of Genesis describes famines in Canaan and shows how they were relieved only by buying Egyptian grain.)

The overriding importance of the annual flood led the Egyptians to reconsider their calendar system. The Sumerians counted the passage of time by numbering the periods from new moon to new moon (months). There were twelve and a fraction of these lunar periods in the cycle of the seasons (year), so that a year was built up, sometimes of 12 months and sometimes of 13 according to an intricate system that kept the years even with the seasons over the long run.

The precision of the calendar was important to farmers, who needed to know when to plant their grain and when to harvest it. Most of the ancient civilizations, including the Jews and Greeks, followed the Sumerians, and the Jewish liturgical year uses the Sumerian system to this day.

The Egyptians, however, considered the Nile flood to be all-important and realized that it came on the average at intervals of 365 days. They therefore made that period the year, and divided it into twelve months of thirty days each, paying no attention to the phases of the moon. In this system, there were five extra days that belonged to no month. This solar calendar may have been worked out some time about 2800 B.C., and with some modifications it is the standard form that is used today.

The prosperity of the Egyptian nation meant that the labor of many people could be siphoned off into nonproductive activities without endangering the production of ample supplies of food and other necessities. Large public works could be undertaken to show the greatness and feed the vanity of the monarch—and of the nation.

These projects would also serve to impress, suitably, both foreigners and future generations. The Egyptian rulers built elaborate palaces for themselves. In fact, they were eventually dubbed *Pharaohs*, which is the Greek version of an Egyptian word meaning "big house."

The rulers also began building more and more elaborate tombs for themselves, and these became truly monumental in the reign of Zoser, the first king of the Third Dynasty, who came to power about 2650 B.C. He built a large pile of stones, set up in six successively smaller stages, one above the other. This monument still exists, and is, in fact, the oldest existing structure in the world.

Zoser's successors built still larger tombs with smooth sides in the shape of square-based pyramids. The climax of pyramid building occurred with Kufu (Cheops, to the Greeks) of the Fourth Dynasty. About 2530 B.C., he supervised the construction of the Great Pyramid, the largest of all such projects. When it was finished, it rose to a height of 481 feet. Its base was 755 feet on each side, and it covered an area of 13 acres. It was composed of 2,300 blocks of stone that weighed, on the average, 2 1/2 tons each.

Great Pyramid of Cheops built

The pyramid-building mania faded after this peak of effort, along with Egyptian power. This diminution of Egyptian power came about because of internal problems. In any realm, there is always a certain tension between the central ruling power of the king and that of the various subrulers (the nobility) who govern the various sections of the land in the king's name.

When a weak king sits on the throne, the nobles are almost certain to take over the power in their own districts and ignore the dictates of the king. These usurpations further weaken the king, and the move toward decentralization of power accelerates. A period in which the nobles are powerful and the central ruler is weak is sometimes called a period of *feudalism*, from an old German word for "property," because the power of the nobility depends on the land they control.

In general, history shows that a nation under a strong central power is better off economically and stronger militarily, than when it is feudal. Under feudalism, endless struggles among the nobility sap the strength of the country.

After 2200 B.C., Egypt passed through nearly two centuries of such a feudal period, until a king of the Eleventh Dynasty, Mentuhotep II, was able to reestablish the power of the central government. In 2000 B.C., Mentuhotep's son and successor Mentuhotep III held the throne, and Egyptian power increased once again.

During this period, Sumeria was not so fortunate as Egypt. At first, it was able to parallel the Egyptians' success. Sumeria had a population of about 1.25 million and ample food supplies. Its largest city, Uruk, compared well with Egypt's Memphis.

The Sumerians also built elaborate temples of brick called ziggurats. These were not as large as the Egyptian pyramids, but were more impressive in other ways, with their outer stairways, which priests could ascend to sacrifices and rituals at the top. (The biblical tale of the Tower of Babel refers to the building of a tall ziggurat, and the tale of Jacob's dream of angels ascending and descending a ladder stretching from Earth to Heaven may also have been inspired by such a structure.)

Great Flood in Tigris-Euphrates Valley

However, Sumerian prosperity received a rude setback as the result of a natural disaster—the first we know of, but by no means the last, to disrupt a civilization. About 2800 B.C., the Euphrates and Tigris rivers flooded. Rivers flood on occasion, and river civilizations have to learn to live with that fact, but this one was a monstrous disaster. Judging by the silt it left behind, which was found and described by Leonard Woolley, the flood may have covered virtually all of Sumeria to heights of as much as twenty-five feet.

Thousands of Sumerians died in the flood and property damage must have been incalculable. It would have taken a long time for Sumeria to recover, and during that time Egypt took an undisputed lead in the rivalry between the two civilizations.

To the Sumerians who lived through the flood, it must have seemed (given their limited geographical knowledge) that the whole world was covered, and that it was a universal deluge. Legends concerning the flood arose in an ever more exaggerated form. We know it best in the version involving Noah that is found in the biblical book of Genesis.

In the aftermath of the flood, the Sumerian cities had a chance to reorganize. This was disastrous, because without the settled boundaries that prevailed before the flood wiped them out, each city tried to grab as much as it could. As a result, warfare began among them, with no one city able to win more than temporary control.

A union with a minimum of fighting, such as had taken place in Egypt some centuries earlier, seemed impossible in Sumeria. Egypt, after all, was protected by desert areas to the east and west, by the sea to the north, and tropical forests to the south. As a result, its population became culturally homogeneous and secure, without fear of invasion from the outside. Sumeria was less well situated, always being vulnerable to invasion by nomadic tribes to the east or west.

Sometime before the flood, a group of people called Akkadians drifted into the Tigris-Euphrates Valley along the northern fringes of Sumeria. They came from the Arabian peninsula to the west and spoke a language entirely unrelated to Sumerian. The Akkadian language was one of a group that we call Semitic today, because the people who speak it are described in the Bible as having been descended from Shem, the oldest son of Noah.

Akkadians enter Tigris-Euphrates Valley

The Akkadians adopted certain aspects of Sumerian culture. They took up the Sumerian system of writing, for instance, and modified it to make it suitable for their own language.

Nevertheless, the Akkadians were *not* Sumerians and did not feel akin to them. They introduced an alien factor in the region and must have been grimly satisfied to see the Sumerian cities fighting one another, weakening all of them.

Indeed, about 2340 B.C., a vigorous Akkadian ruler named Sargon succeeded in defeating the armies of these cities and in taking over all of Sumeria. He also conquered Elam to the east and lands to the northwest and west. Eventually, he ruled over territory that stretched from the Mediterranean Sea in the west,

Sargon creates first empire

to the Caspian Sea in the north, and the Persian Gulf in the south. It included all the civilized regions of western Asia.

Sargon's victories were probably made by advances in military technology. The Sumerians used lances for thrusting, but Sargon's soldiers used lances for throwing, as well as bows and arrows. This meant that his armies could fight effectively at a distance and maul his enemies before they could even close in for an attack.

Sargon was the first great conqueror in history, and he set a pattern that persisted for a long time. He ruled people who were not uniform in language and culture, but made up a heterogeneous realm, so that they were not a nation in the sense that Egypt was. When a ruler achieves supremacy over people of varying cultures, he has established an empire (or *imperium* in Latin, from their word "imperator," used for a military leader). Sargon was the first empire-builder, the first "imperialist."

The Akkadian Empire continued to flourish under Sargon's immediate successors and reached its peak under Sargon's grandson, Naram-Sin, who reigned from 2281 to 2254 B.C.

Empires, however, tend to be unstable. One group of people (in this case, Akkadians) rules over others. Those who are ruled resent it and strive to overthrow the rulers. Much of the strength of the empire, therefore, must be expended on suppressing revolts.

Furthermore, nomadic tribes along the borders of the empire are always likely to invade in search of loot. Usually, the better organized and more advanced technology of the empire can defeat such raids, but all too often the submerged nationalities refuse to fight or even make common cause with the tribal incursion, and the empire, trying to counter both force from abroad and disaffection from within, may topple.

The Akkadian Empire came to an end in this way, about 2180 B.C., less than forty years after the death of Naram-Sin. The fall of the Akkadian Empire allowed the Sumerian cities to recover and control their own destinies once more. In 2000 B.C., the Akkadian Empire was but a fading memory and the leading city was Ur, which was now at the height of its power.

According to Hebrew legend, Abram (later Abraham) the founder of the Israelite nation, was a native of Ur, and about 2000 B.C. he left the city to travel westward to Canaan.

While Egypt and Sumeria held preeminence as the two super-powers of this time, other civilizations were also beginning to make their presence known. The island culture of Crete was one of these.

Crete held a unique place among the civilizations of this period in being located on a comparatively small island rather than on a section of a large continent. This meant Crete had to pay much greater attention to travel by water than either Egypt or Sumeria.

To be sure, both Egypt and Sumeria had rivers as their means for communicating among city-states and for the transportation of goods, but rivers are comparatively tame bodies of water. The banks are always within reach and it is impossible to get lost.

The Mediterranean Sea, on which Egypt borders, and the Persian Gulf, on which Sumeria borders, are considerably more formidable. On those vast stretches of water, it is almost inevitable that one moves out of sight of land. Without guiding land-marks, one might have no way of reaching the desired destination. What's more, storms at sea are deadlier than storms on a river, and the crew of a foundering ship, which might scramble to land from some point out in a river, was not necessarily able to do so when out at sea.

Sea travel was, however, essential, as when the Egyptians (who inhabited a treeless land) imported cedarwood from the Canaanite coast. Carrying the huge logs on shipboard over water was infinitely easier than dragging them overland. On such occasions, however, the Egyptian ships kept as close to land as they could, skimming along the shore from Egypt to Canaan and back.

In order to trade with Egypt, Crete, set in the middle of the Mediterranean Sea, had to develop ships that could sail across a couple hundred miles of water to the African coast, which could then be followed to Egypt. To the north, fortunately, there was a series of islands so closely spaced that ships were never far from any one of them.

As a result, Crete was able to learn from Egypt and develop an

Egyptian-influenced civilization of its own. Cretan civilization is termed Minoan, from Minos, the name of a king of Crete in the Greek myths. Crete was able to spread its Minoan civilization among the islands of the Agean Sea to the north and even to the Greek mainland.

Since the civilizations in Egypt and Sumeria did not have the kind of ships that would enable them to reach Crete in force, the island did not fear invasion. Its city-states, sharing the same culture, could peacefully unite into a nation, and the individual cities remained unwalled.

By controlling the trade of the eastern Mediterranean, Crete prospered, and by 2000 B.C. it had established the first thalassocracy (from Greek words meaning "rule of the seas") in which power rested with a navy rather than with an army.

Indus River civilization in India at its peak

By 2000 B.C., the Indus River civilization was also at its peak. Two cities have been excavated at the sites of Mohenjo-Daro on the lower Indus River, and at Harappa, farther upstream. Both cities were built in a checkerboard pattern, with brick houses, a central citadel on a hill, and surrounding farms with an extensive canal system. The Indus River civilization evolved in isolation, however, and had little influence on the distant Sumerians, and even more distant Egyptians.

Around 2000 B.C., a group of people known as Hittites moved into Asia Minor. Their language was unrelated to the Semitic tongue spoken by the Akkadians, or by the modern Arabs. It was, rather, one of a group of languages that we call Indo-European, because such languages are spoken today in India, Iran, and almost all of Europe. The Hittites are the first people speaking an Indo-European language to enter the stage of history.

As our survey moves rapidly toward the time of Christ, then, we can see major changes occurring all over the globe. Most regions have now experienced a version of the city-state form of government, and the first empire has come into being. The pyramids have been built, boasting of the power of earthly rulers, and the flood has come, reminding people that nature still reigns supreme.

Perhaps most important is that as inventions and innovations piled up over the previous millennia, humans were able once again to double their population. By 2000 B.C., the world population is estimated to have been about 27 million.

World population at 27 million

1000 B.C.

T HIS MILLENNIUM WAS A TIME WHEN HUMAN SOCIETY BEGAN to increase its pace of change around the world. Major, diverse inventions—the chariot, iron, coins, the alphabet— combined to bring great changes in the relationships between nations and people. Empires rose and fell, populations grew, and knowledge expanded dramatically. In every region of the world, humanity entered a time of multiple new developments.

A Gathering Momentum

It was a time, too, when people sought stability, and the question of how best to govern a society became critical. The monarchical form remained primary, but the issue of whether kings ought to be strong or relatively weak was not yet settled. Where possible, many societies sought to increase their own security by creating empires and dominating their neighbors. However, these arrangements usually contributed to greater insecurity in the long run.

As in our own time, the growing human facility with technology was as often applied to achieving military advantage as to improving the quality of life within a society.

Let's look, now, at how these trends and others played themselves out in various regions of the world.

First, Egypt's long period of peace ended because the Indo-European tribes of central Asia put their recently tamed horses to a new use. They trained them to drag a light chariot with large wheels, with one man holding the reins and controlling the horse, while another carried a spear or bow and arrows. The early chariots were little more than a wheeled platform on which two men could stand, but it amounted to a revolutionary new weapon.

In a battle, a racing cloud of these charioteers would be seen bearing down on the foot soldiers of the civilized regions. The foot soldiers usually broke and ran, and the racing charioteers would overtake them, spear them, trample them, and wipe them out. The charioteers spread against all the civilized regions and soon dominated them.

About 1720 B.C., the charioteers reached Egypt by crossing the arid Sinai Peninsula. It would have been a difficult journey on foot, but the speeding horses took it in stride and Egypt's long isolation was over.

Charioteers conquer Egypt

The charioteers (called Hyksos by the Egyptians) met little opposition. They easily defeated the Egyptians, who had no response to counter the new technology. The Hyksos began ruling over northern Egypt and adopted Egyptian culture. It may have been at this time that certain Canaanites entered Egypt and were treated well by the Hyksos. This incident may have given rise to the biblical tales of Joseph and his brothers.

Upriver in the city of Thebes, however, the Egyptians retained their power and gradually learned how to use horse-drawn chariots themselves. By 1570 B.C., the Egyptians, under Ahmose, a ruler of the Eighteenth Dynasty, had driven the Hyksos out of the land that they had ruled for a century and a half. The Egyptians pursued the Hyksos through the Sinai and into Canaan, which they took as a protective buffer against future invasions.

Now Egypt ruled over people who were not Egyptian, and therefore established an empire. Its territory extended far up the Nile and into Asia, almost as far as the Euphrates. Under Tuthmosis III, who reigned from 1504 to 1450 B.C., the Egyptian Empire reached its peak with a population of perhaps 3 million.

The reign of Amenophis IV, who ruled from 1379 to 1362 B.C., marked a turning point. Rulers continued to assert their legitimacy based on connections with the gods, and this meant that a leader's power was to some extent proportional to the power of his or her divinity. Amenophis attempted to align himself with a single god that he considered to be more powerful than all the other gods of the society at that time.

Reign of Akhenaton begins in Egypt

He is the first historical figure who was an avowed monotheist. Amenophis believed in a single god—in his case, the Sun-god, or Aton. He renamed himself Akhenaton ("servant of Aton") and founded a new capital between Memphis and Thebes, which he called Akhetaton ("place of power of Aton"). The priestly caste fought him, as did the people, who wanted their old gods and old ways. While this struggle went on, the borders of the empire were neglected, resistance to invading tribesmen diminished, and the Egyptian Empire began to decline.

Succeeding rulers of the Nineteenth Dynasty arrested the society's descent to some extent. The most famous of these was Rameses II, who reigned from 1304 to 1237 B.C. and struggled to extend the empire's borders in Asia. In the process, he fought a great battle against the Hittites in 1298 B.C., one that weakened both nations. (By tradition, Rameses II is the pharaoh under whom the Israelites were enslaved and in whose court Moses grew to manhood. However, there is no evidence, outside the Bible, to support this.)

In fact, the very effort to maintain an empire forcefully and vigorously sometimes serves to weaken it all the more rapidly. The nation, even if victorious, grows war-weary. A large share of the seasoned soldiers have died in battle and the defeated nations continue to rebel, held in line only at ever-greater cost and with ever-greater difficulty. A puncturing of that shell anywhere is likely to bring the whole structure down. Rameses II, in his strenuous foreign policy, had brought the Egyptian Empire to that point. (It was in the weakened reign of his successor Merneptah that the Israelite exodus under Moses is supposed to have taken place. Again, only the Bible confirms this story.)

Rameses III of the Twentieth Dynasty ruled Egypt from 1188 to 1156 B.C., and in his reign he had to face another group of turbulent invaders, whom the Egyptians called the "people of the sea." With a supreme effort, the Egyptians defeated these invaders, but the strain of doing so finally wore them down. In 1000 B.C., Egypt, having survived two invasions and having spent three centuries as the largest and most powerful empire on Earth, had receded to the position of a minor power, with the feeble monarchs of the Twenty-First Dynasty in control.

After 2000 B.C., the Sumerian civilization, still reeling from the impact of the flood, rapidly declined and passed from the pages of history. New invaders took over the Tigris-Euphrates Valley, adopting Sumerian culture and adding elements of their own. A tribe known as the Amorites, speaking a Semitic language, took over a small Akkadian town named Bab-ilum (Akkadian for "gate of God") about 1800 B.C., and made it their capital. It became a prominent settlement and to the Israelites it was Babel, while to the Greeks it was Babylon. From this town, the lower portion of the Tigris-Euphrates became known as Babylonia, and as of this period we can speak of Sumeria no more.

Reign of Hammurabi begins; written law code developed

Hammurabi ruled as king of Babylon from 1728 to 1686 B.C. and spread his rule over all of Babylonia. He is remembered in history chiefly because of a stone pillar dating back to his reign that still exists and is enscribed with a law-code.

The development of this written law-code was a significant step for human society. At first the laws of a society are simply its customs and traditions, and people refer to the elders for guidance as to what those customs and traditions might be. Dissatisfaction with this approach was bound to grow, since memory is imperfect and there was always the suspicion that those who ruled a land would remember the laws in such a way as to benefit themselves. Eventually, people would demand a *written* law-code, and the Code of Hammurabi is one of the oldest known examples. It is certainly the oldest that we have in its complete original form.

In the upper portion of the Tigris-Euphrates Valley, the Amorites founded another kingdom with its capital at the Akkadian city of Ashur. The kingdom itself was also known as Ashur, and the later Greeks called it Assyria, a name that came to be applied to the upper portion of the Tigris-Euphrates Valley.

Assyria was under the domination of Babylonia in Hammurabi's time. About 1530 B.C., however, the entire valley was conquered by charioteers from the north, a group called Kassites in the later histories.

Generally, invading tribesmen adopt the cultures of the civilized areas they conquer, as the Hyksos adopted Egyptian culture. Sometimes, however, there is a lag and the civilization of the conquered area experiences a decline under the rule of the previously uncivilized tribespeople. Technology, art, and literature all regress, and there is what we call a dark age. After the fall of Hammurabi's empire to the Kassites, a dark age prevailed in the Tigris-Euphrates Valley for over two centuries.

Assyria recovered first. At least, it grew strong enough to engage in periodic wars of conquest. Under its king, Tukulti-Ninurta I, who ruled from 1245 to 1208 B.C., Assyria initiated a policy of waging war with deliberate frightfulness to sap the will of its enemies and have them half defeated before the battle began. Under Tiglath-Pileser I, ruling from 1116 to 1078 B.C., a powerful Assyrian empire was established that ruled the entire Tigris-Euphrates Valley.

After Tiglath-Pileser's death, however, tribesmen called Arameans and Chaldeans overran the valley. By 1000 B.C., then, both Babylonia and Assyria found themselves in the grip of a second dark age.

During this period, certain charioteer tribesmen called Hurrians settled down west of Assyria, in the eastern and southeastern portion of Asia Minor, founding the kingdom of Mittani. To their west, most of Asia Minor was now a part of a strong Hittite kingdom, with its first notable ruler, Labarnas I (*1680–1650 B.C.*).

The Hittites, under their king Suppiluliumis (*1380–1346 B.C.*) defeated and eventually absorbed Mittani. Now there was a Hittite empire, which attempted to expand southward into the area we call Syria; there they met the Egyptians under Rameses II. While the Hittites did well in that battle, they were fatally weakened.

The invaders known as the people of the sea by the Egyptians ravaged Asia Minor and Egypt, and by 1200 B.C. they had put an end to the Hittite kingdom.

Before the Hittites moved off the stage of history, however, they had accomplished an important feat—initiating the Iron Age. Hittites initiate Iron Age

For fifteen hundred years, men had fought with bronze weapons, but a tougher and harder substance was known even then. These were pieces of a gray-black metal that, when beaten into plowshares, swords, knives, or lance-heads, made tools and weapons that were far superior to those made out of bronze. These lumps of metal were actually meteorites composed of an iron-nickel alloy that was unusually hard.

Iron could be formed from rocky ores just as one could form copper and tin. Iron ores, however, required considerably hotter temperatures for smelting, and charcoal was required for the task, rather than wood. Even then, the iron that was formed, without nickel, was not hard enough for the tasks expected of it. Carbon had to be added to make it into steel.

About 1300 B.C., the technique for smelting and carbonizing iron was developed in the foothills of the Caucasus mountain range in northeastern Asia Minor. This was part of the Hittite Empire and the Hittite rulers carefully maintained a monopoly over the new technique because they recognized its importance in war weapons.

This development marked the beginning of the Iron Age, because once the Hittite Empire was destroyed, their monopoly was broken, and the use of iron began to spread to other cultures after about 1200 B.C.

Siege of Troy

In the far northwest of the peninsula, the city of Troy had grown rich through its control of the narrow straits (now known as the Dardanelles and the Bosporus, or simply as "the Straits") through which trade had to pass between the Greek cities of the Aegean Sea and the grain-growing lands north of the Black Sea. The Greeks felt that they could reduce their costs by controlling the Straits themselves. They therefore laid siege to Troy, took it and destroyed it, about 1200 B.C.

The siege of Troy may not have been much of an event at the time, but some centuries later, the Greek poet, Homer, told about it in the *Iliad* and the *Odyssey*, and made it monumentally famous for all time. (According to Homer the Trojan War had nothing to do with economics but was fought over Helen, the wife of the Greek king Menelaus. She had, Homer asserted, "the face that launched a thousand ships.")

After 1200 B.C., there were no long-established powers in Asia Minor. A new group of tribesmen, the Phrygians, filtered in from southeastern Europe, filled the vacuum and established a new kingdom. By 1000 B.C., the Hittites along with Mittani and Troy were gone, and the new kingdom of Phrygia was flourishing. Its wealth impressed the Greeks, who seemed to be chronically poor, and in their myths they spoke of a Phrygian king named Midas, who had the "golden touch."

Crete stood at the peak of its power during this period, dominating the Aegean Sea and its coastlines. By 1600 B.C., invading tribes from the north entered the land we now call Greece, and they were the people we call Greeks. They called the land Hellas, and themselves Hellenes. The name Graecia was first used by the Romans, and that became Greece in modern times.

The Greeks' chief city was Mycenae, in the northeast corner of the Peloponnesus, the southernmost peninsula of Greece; they are therefore called the Mycenean Greeks. At its height, however, Crete held the Myceneans in subjection. From this period, we have the well-known Greek legends of Crete demanding hostages annually from Athens until the legendary Mycenean hero Theseus of Athens ended the subjugation.

However, Crete, like Sumeria before it, suffered a vast natural catastrophe that abruptly halted its development. The island of Thera lay about ninety miles north of Crete, and was the center of a flourishing Minoan civilization. Unfortunately, the island happened to be the top of a volcano rising from the sea, but it showed no signs of activity and no one suspected that it posed a danger.

Then about 1500 B.C. it exploded with a thunderous roar, the most violent volcanic explosion that is known to have happened in historic times. A rain of ashes fell on Crete and tsunamis (tidal waves) struck its shores. The tsunamis also crashed on the shores of Greece, which may have given rise to Greek legends concerning a great flood. Where Thera had once stood, there was only a ring of islets about the open sea. Thera seemed to have vanished beneath the waters, and it was this event that may have been the origins of the Greek legend of Atlantis.

Eruption of Thera; decline of Cretan civilization

The explosion and its aftermath greatly weakened Crete, and the Minoan civilization tottered to a premature end not long afterward. By 1300 B.C., the Mycenean Greeks were in control of Crete and Greece itself. However, the capture of Troy was the last important accomplishment of the Mycenean Greeks. As part of the series of tribal invasions that had sent Egypt into decline and destroyed the Hittite Empire, a new group of Greek-speaking tribes, the Dorians, now invaded Greece. They carried iron weapons that had been picked up from the wreckage of the Hittite Empire, and the bronze-using Myceneans could not stand against them.

The Dorians took over the southern and eastern Peloponnesus, including the old Mycenean city of Sparta, the legendary home of Helen over whom the Trojan War was supposedly fought. They also took over Argos, the city of the Homeric hero, Diomedes, and the island of Crete. Over time, Mycenae itself sank into decay and disappeared as a historical force.

A number of pre-Dorian Greeks, the Ionians, survived in eastern Greece, notably in Athens. Other Ionians fled the mainland and settled on the Aegean islands and the coast of Asia Minor. The central portion of that coast therefore came to be known as Ionia.

Greece and Tigris-Euphrates Valley enter Dark Age

In 1000 B.C., then, the Cretan and Mycenean civilizations were gone and Greece like the Tigris-Euphrates Valley had entered into its own dark age.

The Canaanites were subjected to a series of invasions during this period. They were overrun and controlled by the Hyksos first, then by the Egyptian Empire. When the people of the sea smashed into Egypt, they also landed on the southern Canaanite shores about 1200 B.C. There they established the city-states that made up Philistia. It was these Philistines, speaking an Indo-European language, who gave Canaan its Greek name of Palestine.

We also know the Philistines as enemies of the Israelites from the stories of the Bible. The Israelites invaded Canaan from the west, taking over the Canaanite interior. According to biblical legend, the Israelites had come to Canaan after escaping from Egyptian slavery.

Those Canaanites who retained their independence were confined to the northern coast of their land, around such cities as Tyre, Sidon, and Byblos, and they were best known by their Greek name of Phoenicians. They could flourish in their diminished territory only by trade, and became the first people in the Mediterranean area to venture into the open sea, far from land. They far outdid the Cretans in this respect because the Cretans had, for the most part, been content with scuttling from island to island.

The Phoenicians may have accomplished this feat by learning how to tell directions on clear nights. They saw, as we do, that the sun rises in the east and sets in the west, and that when it is high in the sky in the middle of the day it is always in the south. From this knowledge, one can navigate on sea as well as on land. However, what does one do at night when the sun is not visible?

The Phoenicians seem to have been among the first to notice that by night the highly noticeable seven-star configuration of the Big Dipper was always in the north. That meant that if it were kept on the right hand, the ship was moving westward, while if it were kept on the left hand, the ship was moving eastward. By 1000 B.C., the Phoenicians, using this system, were scouring the length of the Mediterranean Sea, becoming the great traders of the ancient world.

The necessity of trade brought about another great advance. It built on the Sumerian invention of writing and made it possible for you to read this book thousands of years later. Located as it was between Babylonia with its complicated cuneiform writing and Egypt with its equally complicated hieroglyphic writing, Phoenicia found that it could not trade easily unless it could handle both languages. Life would be far easier if they could work out a simple writing code.

Others had made attempts in this direction as early as 1400 B.C. but without complete success. By 1000 B.C., however, the Phoenicians had an alphabet, each letter representing a consonantal sound. Using this alphabet, *any* language could be written down simply.

Phoenicians invent alphabet

Writing was developed independently in a variety of places: Sumeria, China, and southern Mexico, for instance. The alphabet, however, was developed only once—by the Phoenicians. All alphabets in use today, however different they may seem, are clearly descended from that of the Phoenicians.

When the Israelites invaded Canaan in 1200 B.C., they took Jericho, which has existed for nearly seven thousand years as a city. In a battle made famous by the biblical story of Joshua and the trumpeters, the Israelites destroyed Jericho, at least temporarily. For some time after, the Israelites dominated the Philistines of the coast.

Eventually, the Philistines were able to suppress the Israelites, using iron weapons that their adversaries lacked. But about 1000 B.C. the Israelites obtained iron weapons for themselves. David, a leader of the southern tribe of Judah, rose rapidly within the Israelite nation and eventually succeeded to the throne after King Saul. He was able to defeat the Philistines decisively, after which little is heard from them.

David went on to establish an Israelite empire that extended from Egypt in the south to the upper Euphrates in the north. The Israelite population at the time may have been about three hundred thousand, which was not enough to support even an empire as small as David's. It existed only because both the Tigris-Euphrates Valley and Asia Minor remained mired in a deep dark age, and Egypt was still quite weak.

David's empire began to collapse as soon as one of the surrounding areas recovered its strength and was able to revolt. Though the empire was short-lived, its memory remained in the consciousness of the tribe of Judah (the Jews) forever after, with important consequences to the world in general.

Aryans invade India

The charioteers, who had wreaked so much havoc elsewhere, invaded India by 1500 B.C. and put an end to the Indus civilization, which may have had a population of 1 million at its peak. The invaders of India called themselves Aryans, from their word for "noble," and they spoke an Indo-European language known as Sanskrit.

By 1000 B.C., these Indo-European tribes were spreading down the Ganges River and had begun to dominate the life of the great subcontinent. Like the other regions of the world, India entered into a period of rapid change.

China enters Bronze Age

China had entered the Bronze Age about 1500 B.C. and was ruled at that time by the Shang dynasty, the first truly historical dynasty of that nation. China had developed its own system of writing, independently, using an approach that was just as complex as that of the Sumerians and Egyptians. The Chinese, however, never adopted an alphabet, and their writing remains extraordinarily complex to this day, with thousands of characters instead of words made up of letters.

By 1000 B.C., the Chou dynasty had replaced the Shang dynasty. At this time, the importance of the nobles was growing, as China had become a feudal society and remained that way for centuries. China managed to remain somewhat isolated from much of the change sweeping other regions of the world. Nevertheless, China led the world in one category then, as it does now—population.

China's population had grown to well over 5 million at this time, so that it was more populous than any individual kingdom in the west. China contained about one-fifth of all the people on the planet then, and this has continued to be the proportion right down to the present.

China's population at 5 million

By 1000 B.C., refugees from Asia Minor, who were fleeing the Phrygians, reached the western shores of Italy. They were later known as Etruscans, and they represented the first known civilization in Italy. Their language has never been deciphered, and for that reason we know little about them compared to their successors, the Romans.

Civilization was also arising in the Americas, where the Olmecs had begun to build their cities. Elsewhere, the tendency to explore continued to spread the human presence to distant corners of the planet. In the Pacific Ocean, people from southeast Asia were spreading out to nearby islands; the process went on until the Polynesians, as they came to be called, had colonized all the far-flung bits of land in the Pacific. They traveled thousands of miles in their small boats, a feat of seamanship that, given their level of technology, was the most remarkable the world would ever see.

Thus the millennium that stretched from 2000 to 1000 B.C. was a remarkable time, a harbinger of the rapid evolution of human society that would eventually take hold and persist into the future. No nation or empire was safe, as the charioteer tribes roamed the world, bringing down old civilizations and raising new ones in their place. People invented many new things, including monotheistic religions, written legal systems, money, and weapons of iron. All of these innovations, and others, served to maintain humanity's momentum toward the future.

The Bronze Age passed into the Iron Age, and a hard time it was for many who endured it. Natural disasters, such as the volcanic eruption at Thera, continued to play a major role in history by slowing down or even stopping the development of key societies. Civilizations such as the Sumerians, who had dominated the previous millennium, sank out of historical sight, to be replaced by new, more dynamic societies.

As we approach the final millennium before Christ, it is not surprising if we might feel a sense of expectation and possibility, and wonder whether our ancestors sensed it, too.

CHAPTER FOUR

ANNO DOMINI

1 B.C./A.D. 1

(*Author's Note:* In having the sections of this book focus on thousand-year intervals, it should now be possible to go from 1000 B.C. to 0 B.C. There is, however, no year given the number zero; when our current system of counting years was established, Europe was still using Roman numerals, which had no symbol for zero. We can only mark the deficiency by labeling this section 1 B.C./A.D 1, with the slash standing for the missing zero, since that is the only way to truly mark the transition from B.C. to A.D. In addition, so much is now happening worldwide that it is necessary to review events region by region, rather than millennium by millennium.)

I T SEEMS HARD TO AVOID CHARACTERIZING THIS PERIOD AS "the Rise of Empires," because it was the time when Rome rose to prominence, one of the most successful empires ever. However, Rome was not the only empire of the time, as many nations and leaders (such as Alexander the Great) attempted to extend their control over ever-larger domains. Advances in technology continued to be put at the service of these conquerors, aiding them in their belief that they might rule the world.

It should also be kept in mind that this millennium produced the Athenian democracy, a shining example of that political form and a standard against which modern democracies are measured today.

This was also a time in which philosophy and religious thought made great advances. Again, Athens was at the forefront of the former, with thinkers such as Plato and Aristotle illuminating the intellectual landscape. In the meantime, the Middle East and Asia Minor continued to be dominant areas for the latter, producing the new religion of Zoroastrianism and new claims for the importance of the Jews' God, Yahweh.

Then, of course, it is also the last period in which we can speak of the time "before Christ." Regardless of one's views of Jesus' importance as a religious figure, it remains the case that his birth became a pivotal point in our perspective on history.

Western Asia Rebounds

THE DARK AGE FINALLY LIFTED OVER THE TIGRIS-EUPHRATES Valley, and Assyria recovered from its steep decline. Once again, after 900 B.C. the Assyrians proceeded on their career of conquest, carried out with sadistic frightfulness. They were assisted in their task by two new advances in military technology.

First, Assyria learned to make the fullest possible use of iron in warfare. For the first time, an army was completely "ironized," every soldier being equipped with high-caliber iron spears, swords, and shields. In addition, the Assyrians learned how to mount and control a horse. As a result, the importance of the chariot began to diminish—mounted cavalry, faster and more maneuverable, became the new standard.

Under Tiglath-Pileser III, who reigned from 745 to 727 B.C., Assyria finally reached the Mediterranean Sea, conquering Syria in the process. Under his successors Shalmaneser V (726–722 B.C.) and Sargon II (722–705 B.C.), Israel was also overwhelmed and its peoples scattered. The only remaining remnant of David's empire that was left with some degee of independence was his own tribe of Judah.

Then, Judah was attacked by Sennacherib (705–681 B.C.) in 701 B.C. Jerusalem did not fall to the attackers, but Judah was forced to agree to become a tributary of Assyria's. The next Assyrian monarch, Esarhaddon, (680–659 B.C.) attacked and conquered Egypt, so that in 670 B.C., the Assyrian Empire was at the peak of its power and was the largest, mightiest realm that western Asia had yet seen.

Assyria's capital Nineveh had been established by Sennacherib and became the largest city on Earth. Under Esarhaddon's successor, Asshurbanipal, it was further beautified and enlarged. Asshurbanipal built the largest library the world had seen to that time, containing over 22,000 clay tablets.

However, two centuries of almost continuous fighting had worn Assyria down and left it the empty shell that conquering nations often become. There were still unconquered peoples beyond its borders, notably the Medes, living east of Assyria in what is now Iran. In addition, the Chaldeans of Babylonia rebelled constantly against Assyria, and despite repeated defeats threatened to revolt again.

Fifteen years after the death of Asshurbanipal, the Chaldeans within the empire combined with the Medes outside it, and together they stormed and destroyed Nineveh in 162 B.C. The Assyrian Empire could not recover from such a blow, and it faded with astonishing speed. By 600 B.C. the Assyrians were no longer a major force in history.

The Chaldeans then inherited the Tigris-Euphrates Valley and retained control over the Mediterranean coast, but they let Egypt regain its freedom. Then, when the Judeans tried to rebel, the Chaldean monarch Nebuchadnezzar II (630–562 B.C.) took Jerusalem and destroyed its temple. Thus, the line of kings descended from David came to an end.

Nebuchadnezzar's Rule of Chaldean Empire begins

The Chaldean Empire reached its peak under Nebuchadnezzar. His capital of Babylon had now become the largest city in the world. He completed a ziggurat that was the largest of its type, reaching a height of three hundred feet. It had long remained unfinished when Babylon was under Assyrian domination, and that may have given rise to the tale of the unfinished Tower of Babel in the biblical book of Genesis.

He also built an elaborate palace that rose in stages like a ziggurat. On the terrace he planted gardens, which became known as the famous Hanging Gardens of Babylon, later considered to be one of the Seven Wonders of the Ancient World. Nebuchadnezzar may well have ruled over as many as 2 million people, but after his death, his empire lost much of its strength. The lands beyond its borders, relieved of that pressure, now had a chance to begin their development.

In Asia Minor, the Phrygian kingdom had been destroyed by the invasion of Cimmerians, tribesmen from the Ukrainian steppes. In place of the Phrygians there arose, about 680 B.C., the kingdom of Lydia, with its capital at Sardis in western Asian Minor. The Lydians dominated the Greek cities on the Aegean coast of Asia Minor but allowed them to rule themselves.

At this time, a great advance in economic affairs was made, thanks to the Lydians. Metals such as gold and silver were commonly used as media of exchange. They were valuable because they were rare, and this meant that small, easily portable quantities could be exchanged for large amounts of other commodities.

However, each piece of gold or silver had to be weighed during every transaction so that its value could be calculated. This in turn always roused the fear that the scales might be crooked, or that the gold and silver might be intermixed with less valuable metals.

Lydians invent coins   The Lydian kingdom offered the rest of the world a solution, by issuing coins. These were pieces of gold or silver, or an alloy of the two, that were stamped with its weight and value. A coin would carry a picture of the king or some other design that confirmed the coin to be official and confirmed its purity. The use of these coins greatly accelerated trade and substantially added to the wealth of Lydia. (Croesus, who ruled Lydia from 560 to 546 B.C., was so admired for his wealth that the Greeks invented a phrase, "rich as Croesus," to go with their earlier "Midas touch," and both terms are still used today.)

The use of coins spread rapidly throughout the ancient civilized world, because they facilitated commerce greatly. Like many inventions of the past, they are taken for granted in modern times but made an enormous difference when they were first brought into common usage.

West of Lydia and Chaldea lay the Median Empire, stretching out over what is now Iran and Afghanistan. This empire became famous for something that *didn't* happen, an almost-battle with the Lydians that has a special importance to historians. Just as the two armies were about to attack each other, a total eclipse of the sun occurred. Both armies took the event to be a dire warning from the gods, so they broke off the battle and made peace.

Astronomers can calculate backward and determine the day on which this eclipse took place—May 28, 585 B.C. This aborted battle is the first event in all of human history for which the time is known to the exact day.

Eclipse of May 28; first event in history known to exact day of occurrence

The importance of the Medes in history rests even more strongly on the fact that they produced a religious reformer known as Zarathustra (628–551 B.C.). Known as Zoroaster to the Greeks, he preached a new religion that portrayed the universe as being divided between two powers equal in strength and contending for dominance. One was Ahura Mazda, who represented light and goodness. The other was Ahriman, who stood for darkness and evil. According to Zoroaster, the eternal struggle between the two produced no clearcut victory, but the intervention of human beings might swing the result one way or the other.

Birth of Zarathustra, founder of Zoroastrianism

This view, called Zoroastrianism, gradually came to dominate the Median Empire and its successors, and echoes of it can be found in a number of modern-day religions, especially Christianity.

A district in the southwestern portion of the Median Empire proved to be that political system's undoing. Known as Persia to the Greeks, it produced a remarkable young general named Cyrus, who became the Persian ruler in around 558 B.C. Cyrus rebelled against his Median overlord and in 550 B.C., took the Median capital and became ruler of the newly constituted Persian Empire.

Cyrus creates new Persian Empire

Under Cyrus, Persia trod the well-worn road of imperial expansionism. He attacked and absorbed Lydia in 546 B.C., and the

Chaldean Empire in 539 B.C. Cyrus died in 529 B.C. while on an expedition to expand Persia's borders in central Asia. His son, Cambyses, took up the cause and succeeded in conquering Egypt. Cambyses was followed by another strong leader, Darius I (550–486 B.C.), who extended Persian domination into northwestern India and the Thracian regions of Europe north of Greece.

The Persian Empire reached its peak under Darius in 500 B.C. It was by far the largest empire western Asia had yet seen. Its size approached that of the modern United States, and Darius may have ruled over as many as 13 million people.

The Persians, however, also followed the unfortunate pattern of empires by trying to extend their rule against a determined and courageous foe, in this case the Greek city-state of Athens. The Greeks were greatly outnumbered by the Persians, but they were far better organized, and they had something to fight for—a unique way of life in which people were responsible for their own government.

Darius tried first and failed to defeat the Athenians. His son, Xerxes (519–465 B.C.) continued to campaign, but Athens rebuffed him, as well. As a result of these failures, the Persian Empire began to crumble, and the Greeks became a growing danger to them.

Birth of Aristotle

The danger became very real with the advent of Alexander III of Macedon, a Greek-speaking kingdom north of the Greek city-states. Alexander lived a short but eventful life, much of it at the expense of the unfortunate Persians. Between 334 and 324 B.C., he managed to conquer all of the Persian Empire in an astonishing campaign that led to his being called Alexander the Great. Ruling all of Persia and Greece, his own empire reached a population of some 20 million. However, after his death at the early age of thirty-three, his empire rapidly disintegrated, with its fragments being seized by competing generals who previously had served him.

Seleucid Era begins

Most of the Asian dominions fell to Seleucus (356–281 B.C.), whom we discussed earlier in regard to various calendrical systems. He founded a Seleucid empire, and it was from this founding that the so-called Seleucid era counted its years.

The monarchs who succeeded Seleucus (the Seleucids) looked westward toward Greece, neglecting the eastern portions of the empire and giving the native population a chance to break free. For example, the Parthians, living in a distant eastern province of what had been the Persian Empire, had by 248 B.C. made themselves virtually independent of the Seleucids.

The Seleucids struggled for a century to bring Parthia back into the fold, but by 140 B.C. a Parthian ruler named Mithradates I had defeated the Seleucids and taken over the entire Tigris-Euphrates Valley. The Parthian Empire constituted a kind of rebirth of the Persian Empire, controlling the eastern half of the area over which Darius had ruled.

The Parthians grew stronger as the Seleucids declined in power, able to resist the Romans when Roman armies took over what remained of the Seleucid dominions. In 53 B.C., Parthian forces won a great victory over the Roman general, Marcus Licinius Crassus (115–53 B.C.). In 40 B.C., Parthian soldiers even reached the Mediterranean and briefly took Judea.

By 1 B.C./A.D. 1, then, western Asia had witnessed the passing of the Assyrians, Chaldeans, Lydians, Medians, and original Persians. Now it was a battleground between the Romans and the revived Persians, the Parthians. Unlike earlier kingdoms and empires, the Persians had withstood defeat and were still fighting for supremacy in the region.

I N ISRAEL, A RATHER DIFFERENT STORY WAS TAKING SHAPE. *Israel* David's son and successor, Solomon, who reigned from 962 to *Struggles for* 922 B.C., stopped seeking conquests. He chose the rather unique path, for a king of that time, of living in peace and *Identity* becoming known for his wisdom rather than his conquests. He supervised the building of a temple to the god of the Israelites, Yahweh. It was unique for the ancient world because, consistent **Reign of Solomon** with the Jewish heritage, it contained no sculptured representa- **begins** tions of any god figure.

After Solomon's death his kingdom fractured and David's empire disappeared, having existed for fewer than eighty years. The northern tribes, who had always resented Judean domination, broke away and became the kingdom of Israel, with its capital eventually at Samaria. The smaller kingdom of Judah retained Jerusalem as its capital and continued under the successors to David.

The division weakened both kingdoms, and they had the greatest difficulty in retaining their independence against the onslaughts of their neighbors. Both kingdoms tended toward polytheism, but a strong party of monotheists in Judea sought to establish Yahweh as the only God.

Certain Yahvist prophets, such as Amos and Isaiah, functioned as effective propagandists for the monotheistic viewpoint, and their ideas were eventually included as books in the Bible.

When the Assyrians conquered Israel in 722 B.C., its aristocracy was deported into Assyrian dominions. Many legends grew up in later centuries about the ten lost tribes of Israel, but it seems likely that they simply faded into their Assyrian surroundings after the deportations.

Judah survived as an Assyrian tributary and, under Josiah, who reigned from 640 to 609 B.C., Yahwism won a complete victory, at least for a time. A book of Jewish law, supposedly dating back to the time of Moses, was discovered in the temple (it is thought to be the present biblical book of Deuteronomy).

Temple of Jerusalem destroyed
However, Josiah died in battle, and Jerusalem was taken over by Nebuchadnezzar, ruler of Chaldea, in 586 B.C. The temple was destroyed and the most prominent Jews were again carried off into exile.

Unlike the previously deported Israelites, however, these Jews did not lose their national identity. Indeed, they prospered in exile under the relatively tolerant Chaldean rule. In fact it was there, with the leadership of the prophet Ezekiel, that Yahwism won its final victory—the Jewish historical and prophetical writings were all gathered into what we now know as the Bible. The early legends about the creation of the universe, the flood, and the Tower of Babel, clearly show the influences of Chaldean science and culture.

The Jews also tried to tie their history to that of ancient Sumeria by having Abraham come from Ur, as the Romans later tried to tie their history to ancient Greece by having their city's founder, Aeneas, come from Troy.

Once Cyrus of Persia took over Chaldea, he permitted those Jews who wished to do so to return to Judah. There, a new small temple was built in Jerusalem in 515 B.C., and the Jews did their best to reconstruct their old nation, this time under Persian protection. A Persian official of Jewish origin, Nehemiah, supervised the rebuilding of the walls around Jerusalem in 438 B.C., and the scribe Ezra carried out a religious revival that established the importance of the newly edited Bible.

In addition, a nameless prophet, known as "the second Isaiah," preached the *universality* of Yahweh. He preached that not only was Yahweh the only God of the Jews, he was the only God who had ever existed. It was from this second Isaiah that true monotheism was passed on to later Jews, and through them to the Christians and Muslims.

Judea existed peacefully under the Persians and absorbed some of the Zoroastrian mythology, as well. Although they stoutly maintained that God was the sole lord of the universe, the Jews now accepted a principle of evil in the form of Satan. He could not win the war against God, but he did win victories over human beings, which made him an extremely dangerous adversary. In this way, the Zoroastrian principle of the conflict between good and evil entered Judaism, and eventually reached Christianity.

After the death of Alexander the Great, Judea came under the very mild rule of Ptolemy I (365–283 B.C.), who had become king of Egypt. Many Jews migrated into Egypt at this time, and especially into Ptolemy's capital of Alexandria. Under Ptolemy II (308–246 B.C.), a project was undertaken with royal patronage to translate the Bible into Greek. Since seventy scholars were put in charge of the project, the translation was called the *Septuagint*, from a latin word for "seventy."

Bible translated into Greek

By 250 B.C., the Bible could be read by anyone speaking Greek, which meant that it had been opened up to the most advanced civilization on Earth at the time. It was an extremely important step in making Judaism, through its daughter religions, into a worldwide faith. In turn, the basic values of Judaism were disseminated into the societies of the world.

This time of opportunity was short-lived, however. In 198 B.C., Judea passed from the Ptolemies of Egypt to the Seleucids of Syria, who were far less tolerant. Under Antiochus IV (215–164 B.C.), they made a serious attempt to force the Jews to abandon their faith and adopt Greek culture.

Led by Judas Maccabeus and his brothers (the Maccabees) the Jews revolted against the Seleucids in 168 B.C. The Seleucids were too weak to repress the revolt, and Judea finally gained its independence in 151 B.C. under John Hyrcanus I and Alexander Jannaeus.

Maccabean Judea reached a modest peak of power during this time but was eventually brought low by dynastic quarrels and civil war. In 63 B.C., the Roman general Gnaeus Pompeius (106–48 B.C.) took over Judea, making it into a Roman province and appointing Herod (73–4 B.C.) the king of Judea. Herod tried to please the Jews by adhering to Jewish custom and enlarging the temple, but he was an Idumean by birth and was friendly to the Romans, two facts that displeased the more conservative Jewish leaders.

Many Jews, remembering the successful revolt of the Maccabees and heeding the words of their prophets, dreamed of a Messiah (an annointed one) who would be a descendant of David and lead them in a successful revolt against Rome. They expected a secular, as well as religious leader, who would finally free them from foreign domination.

Birth of Jesus (approximate date)

In 1 B.C./A.D. 1, then, the Jews were dreaming of revolution and restlessly searching for the Messiah they expected to come at any moment. At about this time, according to the biblical story, a child was indeed born in Bethlehem who was said to be of Davidic descent, or alternatively the Son of God. He was eventually thought of as Joshua the Messiah or, in Greek, Jesus Christ.

The Phoenicians Flourish, then Falter

THE PHOENICIAN CITIES HAD BEEN CONQUERED BY ASSYRIA, but they successfully resisted the Chaldeans. Later, they again fell under foreign sway when the Persians conquered them.

In spite of their difficulties, the Phoenicians continued their remarkable trading and exploring missions throughout the Mediterranean. By 900 B.C., they may even have ventured out past the Straits of Gibraltar into the Atlantic Ocean. Tin ores were becoming exhausted in western Asia (the first known case of a natural resource being completely depleted) and the Phoenicians may have gone to Cornwall on the southwestern tip of Britain to find new sources. Of course, they kept the location secret in order to preserve their monopoly. They were so successful that to this day we must guess where it was, rather than knowing for certain.

They also founded cities in various parts of the Mediterranean, Cyprus, the north African coast, Sicily, and Spain. Carthage was the most important of their colonies, near modern-day Tunis, and founded according to legend in 814 B.C. However, the political power of the Phoenician cities dissipated under the domination of the Assyrians and Persians. Only Carthage, which was far enough away to be free of foreign influence, grew more powerful.

By 650 B.C., Carthage had its own navy, and thanks to its flourishing commerce, a large army of mercenary soldiers. The city took on the leadership of all the Phoenician colonies and became the dominant force in the western Mediterranean.

The Phoenicians served as the sea-arm of the Persian Empire, and at some time about 500 B.C. they may have succeeded in circumnavigating Africa on a voyage that took them three years. However, when Alexander the Great overthrew the empire, he laid siege to Tyre, a principal Phoenician city, and utterly destroyed it. After that, Phoenician influence ebbed considerably, and only Carthage remained a factor in history.

Carthage had fought the Greeks in Sicily for centuries without either side gaining a decisive victory. However, the Carthaginians soon found themselves facing a new and implacable enemy. In 264 B.C., Rome, which by now was in control of all of Italy, took over the fight from the Greeks. In the first Punic war, which lasted for twenty-three years, Carthage was defeated and lost Sicily to the Romans.

In spite of their setback, the Carthaginians continued to extend their dominions in Spain, and the Romans interceded. Hannibal, one of the most brilliant generals in history, led the Carthaginian forces in Spain, and he seemed able to outmanuever the Romans at will. In 218 B.C., he invaded Italy but surprised the Romans by approaching by land instead of by sea. He marched across southern Gaul (modern France) and clambered his way across the Alps with an army that included many war elephants.

During this second Punic war, Hannibal defeated the Romans in three successive battles, the third at the town of Cannae in 215 B.C. It was one of the worst defeats a Roman army had ever suffered, but they held on grimly against the invading enemy and refused to capitulate.

Hannibal, meanwhile, suffered from lack of support from the Carthaginian rulers in Africa, many of whom feared him more than Rome. In spite of his brilliance, Hannibal could not hope to succeed in his Italian campaign without a secure flow of supplies. In 201 B.C., the Romans managed to defeat him and force a ruinous peace on Carthage.

But, Carthage was a resilient society. Shorn of all its possessions, confined to the boundaries of the city itself, constantly harassed by its neighbors and by Rome, the Carthaginians still regained their prosperity. Fearing a resurgent Carthage, the unforgiving Romans launched a third Punic war in 149 B.C. Although the Carthaginians defended themselves heroically for nearly three years, they were finally wiped out and their city utterly destroyed in 146 B.C.

By 1 B.C./A.D. 1, the Phoenician peoples, who had done so much in Canaan, Tyre, and Carthage, no longer had any influence on the world scene. Like the Sumerians and other cultures before them, they had given much to the world, but that alone did not guarantee their survival.

Greece Invents Democracy

KINGS RULED THE WORLD FROM 1000 B.C. to 1 B.C./A.D. 1, and when they grew stronger they conquered their neighbors and made themselves into emperors. As in the past, these rulers identified themselves with divine powers to reinforce their authority, but as military technology improved, they often relied on pure force to maintain their power.

The inventiveness of human beings was not confined to the physical world, however, and the last millennium before Christ brought forth new innovations in the political realm, as well. Nowhere was this more the case than in Greece.

Greece emerged from the dark age into which it had been thrown by the Dorian invasion as a collection of city-states scattered over the land we now call Greece and along the Aegean shores in Asia. The land was broken up into mountain ranges, and each city-state existed in its own small valley. Geography prevented them from joining into a voluntary union, as had happened in Egypt, for example, but it also provided a mighty obstacle to empire building. Throughout the history of ancient Greece, the city-states never combined together successfully, and empires were short lived. The Greeks put a high value on their freedom, and war among the city-states was perpetual.

The Greeks developed heavily armed infantry (hoplites) trained to fight in unison, supporting and protecting one another. This was a major improvement over the individualistic approach that had prevailed in the time of the Trojan War, and for a time, these were the best fighters in the world. However, the neighbors of the Greeks, who *did* form nations and empires, learned the same martial techniques, providing a threat to the Greeks' freedom that eventually led to their downfall.

The Greeks were not, however, totally disunited. They all felt the common bond of the Greek language, the Homeric poems, and the periodic athletic games that were open to all and conducted in an atmosphere of peace. Of these, the Olympic Games were the most important, the first of which were held (according to tradition) in 776 B.C.

Once out of the dark age the Greek population boomed, reaching a figure of about 2 million by 700 B.C. As in other cases in which overpopulation threatened, this led to a colonization movement, and there was a period when the Greeks went abroad to found colonies on the shores of the Black Sea, in Sicily, southern Italy, and northern Africa. Eventually, colonization stopped because the best sites had been taken and because Carthage and the Asian powers opposed it. Perhaps half a million

Greeks had migrated to the colonies, but the population of the homeland continued to rise.

Sparta and Athens, the two leading city-states of the time, found their own solutions to the population problem. In the south, Sparta fought a long war with neighboring cities and took over all of the Peloponnesus, enslaving the non-Spartan population. Sparta thus became the largest city-state in Greece, but the cost was high.

In order to make sure that the oppressed majority would not revolt, the Spartan minority subjected themselves to a rigorous military regimen. The Spartans turned themselves into military machines and became the best fighters in Greece, but it was at the cost of almost all advances in culture.

Unfortunately, the Spartan example is one that has been followed all too often by societies who have faced similar problems later in history, and it ultimately proved to be an unstable solution.

Athens, located in east-central Greece, took a different approach. The Athenians united to themselves the entire peninsula of Attica, becoming the second largest city-state in Greece. However, their prosperity was built on trade rather than war, and they were able to support a growing population through commerce. In addition, trading all over the eastern Mediterranean and Black Sea introduced the Athenians to a variety of cultures, which laid the groundwork for establishing the most remarkable of Greek societies.

Unlike many other cultures of the time, the Greek cities had abandoned monarchy, for the most part. Sparta did have two kings, but they were primarily military rather than political leaders. However, the cities' initial alternative to monarchy was not much of an improvement. They were governed by a group of noble families, a form of rule known as oligarchy, or "rule of the few."

The common people felt cheated by this arrangement, and they often turned to someone who promised to rule on their behalf. These rulers became kings without having inherited a throne, and were called *tyrants* from the Greek word for "master."

Some of them governed so corruptly that tyrant has now come to mean a cruel or corrupt ruler.

All the tyrants of those days were not truly tyrannical in our terms. Neither their rule nor periodic foreign domination prevented a rapid cultural advancement, which remains a wonder to us today. The Ionian cities on the Aegean coast of Asia Minor, such as Ephesus and Miletus, were dominated by Lydia and Persia, for example, but they still produced a group of thinkers who laid the foundation for the field of western philosophy as we know it.

These thinkers studied the world around them and tried to gain an idea of the laws that governed it, without having to fall back on supernatural explanations for events. This was a revolutionary departure from previous worldviews, which ascribed almost everything to the intervention of the gods or God. While humanity would have to wait for more than a millennium before the true scientific revolution took place, its seeds were sown in the rocky soils of pre-Christian Greece.

According to tradition, Thales of Miletus (625–547 B.C.) was the first of these natural philosophers. He might almost be considered the first scientist known by name, and following his lead the Greeks led the world in developing science and mathematics for a thousand years.

Birth of Thales of Miletus, first natural philosopher

When the Ionian cities rebelled against Persia in 499 B.C., they were crushed and the framework for supporting creative thinking disappeared from that area, as did philosophy. However, as we have seen, ideas are durable and portable, and philosophy reappeared in Athens, where it flourished.

Athens now became an innovator in many fields of human endeavor, spurred on by the inspiration of its resident thinkers. For example, Athens attempted to establish an economic system that was more equitable for all its citizens. Solon (630–560 B.C.) created a system that limited the amount of land that could be owned by the rich and gave the poor a greater say in government. He also reformed the currency to encourage trade and set up a less punitive law-code. Solon accomplished all of these reforms without becoming a tyrant, and he was so admired for his deeds that legislators are still called solons to this day.

Birth of Solon, first "legislator," and early developer of democracy

All of these initiatives moved Athens in the direction of a new political form, called democracy, or rule of the people. Democracy addressed the problem of political legitimacy in a way that was the opposite of monarchy. Kings claimed to derive the right to rule from above, citing their connection with the gods. Democratic leaders at the time of Athens and today claim their right to govern from below, citing the "will of the people."

Many of the Athenians considered democracy to be the ideal form of government, and it did have positive effects. By liberating speech and thought, it enabled the city to lift philosophy, mathematics, science, and literature to a level that has been an inspiration to the Western world ever since.

Not everyone in Athens was a democrat, however. The conservatives of Athens fought Solon's reforms, and the situation deteriorated to the point that Athenians found themselves willing to support a tyrant again.

He was Peisistratus, who ruled Athens almost continuously from 567 to 521 B.C. He was a rather mild tyrant who kept Solon's reforms, protected the peasantry, maintained the peace, and encouraged industry and trade. He even saw to it that the Homeric poems were edited into the versions that we have today. After he died, however, the Athenians expelled his son and reestablished their democracy.

Athens created the first important democracy in the civilized world, but it was not perfect by any means. Citizenship was open only to those of Athenian birth on both sides of the family. Foreigners had only limited rights, and there was a large population of slaves with no rights at all.

Athens also had external problems with which to contend. The city had helped the Ionian cities in their doomed revolt against Persia in 499 B.C., and Darius was determined to punish the Athenians for that. In 490 B.C., he sent an expedition across the Aegean Sea, with a mission to land in Attica and take Athens. (This was the foray discussed earlier in our section on Persia's development.)

The Athenians tried to get Sparta to help them, but the Spartans were cautious and slow to move on any political initiatives. The Athenians were forced to meet the Persians virtually alone at Marathon, twenty-six miles from Athens. There, the well-trained hoplites managed to defeat the numerically superior Persian forces in an upset victory.

Greeks defeat Persians at Marathon

A runner carried the good news to Athens and, ever since, runners have competed in marathons of a distance equal to his original journey.

Xerxes, the son of Darius, sought to realize his father's ambitions, and in 480 B.C. he sent a huge expedition into Greece that seemed certain to carry all before it. However, at the narrow pass of Thermopylae in northern Greece, a small Spartan force of some three hundred men heroically delayed Xerxes, fighting to the last man. The Persians continued their march in spite of the Spartan sacrifices, reached Athens, and burned the city.

The Persian victory proved to be illusory, however. In the ten years since Marathon, the Athenians under the guidance of Themistocles (524–460 B.C.) had built a powerful fleet. The population of Athens had in fact been evacuated to nearby islands and the Athenian fleet, with help from other Greek cities, destroyed the Persian fleet at the Battle of Salamis in September 480 B.C. Then in 479 B.C., the Spartans defeated the Persians in a land battle at Plataea, just north of Athens.

The Persians retreated after Plataea, and from then on it was the Greeks who took the offensive. Athens saw to it that all the Greek cities on the Persian-dominated coast were freed and joined with Athens to form a kind of Athenian Empire. Athens also built walls around the city and its port, Piraeus, with long walls connecting the two cities.

In 460 B.C., a liberal nobleman, Pericles (495–429 B.C.) became the virtual ruler of Athens, and under him the city entered a golden age of literary, artistic, and philosophical achievement.

Pericles rules Athens; "Golden Age" begins

Athens and all of the Greek cities were now at their peak, with a total population of over 3 million. Athens alone had a population of about 50,000 citizens and some 100,000 slaves.

However, the persistent rivalries of the city-states eventually ruined the golden age and Greece itself. Sparta, having helped Athens defeat the Persians, watched Athens' growing strength with jealousy. The Spartans held back for a while, because they habitually moved slowly, but also because Sparta had suffered a serious earthquake in 464 B.C. This disaster all but destroyed the city and encouraged the Spartan slaves to revolt. It took Sparta fifteen years to fully recover, during which time Athens built its walls.

Peloponnesian War begins

Athens unfortunately was not good at empire building. The Athenians were too domineering in their relations with the other cities of the empire, spending the common funds too freely on the beautification of Athens itself. (The Parthenon, perhaps the most beautiful structure ever built, was constructed at this time.) The Greek cities turned to Sparta as a liberating influence, and in 431 B.C. Sparta went to war with Athens, thus initiating the Peloponnesian War.

The Spartans invaded Athenian territory, and the Athenians retreated inside the city's walls. Overcrowding and a lack of sanitary facilities led to a plague that killed many citizens, including Pericles, greatly weakening Athens.

The war lasted twenty-seven years, exhausting both societies. Persia began to pay subsidies to Sparta in return for a promise to let the Persians regain the Greek cities on the coast of Asia Minor, but even this aid did not defeat the Athenians. As long as the Athenian navy remained in existence, Athens was safe. However, Sparta finally found a capable admiral, Lysander, who destroyed the Athenian fleet in 404 B.C. at Aegospotami, not far from the site of ancient Troy. Athens was forced to capitulate, pull down its walls, reestablish oligarchy, and accept Spartan domination.

Birth of Plato

Sparta proved to be as poor a master of others as Athens had been, however. Riding a wave of anti-Spartan sentiment, the Athenians successfully revolted, and had restored her walls and

Alexander the Great begins his conquests

her democracy by 393 B.C. While Athens never regained its previous power, it remained culturally dominant. In spite of the war and hardships, the society produced Plato (428–348 B.C.) and Aristotle (384–322 B.C.), two of the greatest philosophers of all time.

Plato started his academy, the forerunner of the modern universities, and made his mentor Socrates famous through the well-known "Socratic Dialogues" that constituted the bulk of his writings.

In spite of the great contributions made to the world by Athens and the other Greek city-states, their inability to cooperate led to their downfall in the final centuries of this millennium. While Persia had become an empty shell because of its many failed expeditions against the Greeks, the Greeks could not take advantage of their adversary's weakness.

For example, Sparta had dominated the city of Thebes for some time, but Thebes rose against the Spartans under the leadership of Peopidas (d. 364 B.C.) and Epaminondas (410–362 B.C.). Epaminondas had developed a new system in which hoplites were arranged in many columns to form a phalanx (fist) that would destroy any ordinary force that it opposed.

In 371 B.C., the Theban phalanx met the Spartans at Leuctra. The Spartans were too rigid to change tactics in the face of the odd Theban formation, and they were soundly defeated. Only Epaminodas' death in a later battle prevented the Thebans from taking over Sparta itself.

However, the Spartan defeat did not end the internecine warfare, which created a vacuum eventually filled by the Macedonians. Philip of Macedon, Alexander's father, had been a prisoner at Thebes and had seen the phalanx in action. He reorganized the Macedonian army and created a phalanx that was an enormous improvement over the Theban version.

Philip trained his army thoroughly, supported it with cavalry, and made strategic use of catapults and other siege machinery. Gold mines were found on Macedonian territory, and he used them to bribe enemy politicians to his advantage. Philip incrementally increased his strength, and in 338 B.C. he crushed a combined Athenian-Theban army at Chaeronea, west of Thebes.

With that victory, all of Greece and much of Macedonia fell into Philip's hands. It had been his plan to attack Persia, but he was assassinated in 336 B.C., leaving the mission to Alexander, who was then only twenty-one.

We have already recounted how Alexander crushed the Persians, but he actually had to handle the Greeks first, and he was quite adept at the task. When Philip died, Greece and all the other conquered territories rose up against Alexander. However, he proved himself to be a military genius right away, moving with lightning speed and smashing each enemy in turn.

Death of Alexander the Great

Alexander's subsequent conquest of Persia gave him control of the entire civilized world except for Carthage and the Greeks of Italy and Sicily. He never lost a battle during his military career, and we can only guess how the world would have developed if he had lived longer. However, Alexander the Great died in 323 B.C. at the age of thirty-three after a drunken debauch.

The subsequent breakup of Alexander's empire had the salutary effect of spreading Greek language and culture all over the shores of the Mediterranean. Descendants of Alexander's general Antigonus (the Antigonids) took over Macedon and most of Greece itself, while the Seleucids ruled much of Asia, and the Ptolemies controlled Egypt. Taken together, these were all known as the Hellenistic kingdoms.

A brain drain ensued, as enterprising Greeks and Macedonians rushed to the new kingdoms for adventure and profit. This outmigration finally caused a decline in the population of Greece, but it was a precipitous and rather unhealthy drop.

The Greeks, both at home and abroad, never ceased their intellectual endeavors, and science and mathematics remained a Greek monopoly for centuries. However, as we observe how civilizations evolve and develop, it almost seems that they can burn themselves out, with periods of intense activity. In the case of the Greeks, they had more or less depleted their considerable energies by this time. Their culture displayed less creativity and more looking backward to the past. They broke new ground less often and indulged in more commentaries on their brilliant history.

Unfortunately, the new Hellenistic kingdoms inherited the old Greek habit of fighting among themselves. The battles were perpetual and all the kingdoms were weakened as a result. Most of the Seleucid Empire was eventually lost to the Parthians, and everything else was absorbed over time, by Rome.

By the last century B.C., Ptolemaic Egypt was the only Hellenistic kingdom left. It was no longer the Egypt of the pharoahs, but it continued to be remarkably successful. The Nile River supplied copious harvests as it had in the past, and the long-suffering Egyptian people managed to withstand conquest without losing their culture.

Between the Assyrian and Persian conquests, an Egyptian Twenty-Sixth Dynasty ruled the land and revived Egyptian art and literature for a century and a half. Toward the end of the Persian domination, Egypt broke free for fifty years, but was retaken in 343 B.C., and the old Egypt was not independent again until modern times.

Egypt slipped quietly under the rule of Alexander, and it was there that he established what may be his most enduring legacy— the city of Alexandria. Sitting on the western edge of the Nile delta, it slid just as quietly under the rule of the Ptolemies. The first three Ptolemies were capable and benign rulers, and Egypt was better off for a century than it had been since the days of the Egyptian Empire nine hundred years earlier.

Alexandria was, in many ways, the archetype of our modern world cities. It was in Egypt, but not necessarily of it, and all the multicultural currents of the planet swirled through it. The Ptolemies beautified Alexandria and established a museum, or temple dedicated to the Muses, who were considered to be the divine inspiriation for artists and scientists. The museum was the first real approach to the modern university, and through it Alexandria rapidly became the intellectual center of the world.

The Ptolemies founded a library in conjunction with the museum, and it eventually became the largest in the world. At its height, it contained several thousand rolls of papyrus. Unfortunately, the library was destroyed by fire, leaving us bereft of a treasure trove of ancient knowledge.

For a time, Alexandria was not only the largest city in the world but also the most cosmopolitan. In addition to its Greek and Egyptian populations, for example, it contained numerous Jews and other nationalities. The city was also famous for the Pharos, a lighthouse about 440 feet high that stood in Alexandria's harbor. There, a fire was kept burning through the night to guide ships.

The Pharos, like the Hanging Gardens of Babylon, was one of the Seven Wonders of the Ancient World.

By 230 B.C., Ptolemaic Egypt had reached its height and was the most prosperous and strongest nation in the Western world; its population approached 4 million. However, after 221 B.C., when Ptolemy III died, less capable members of the dynasty ruled Egypt and it gradually lost its vigor. Early on, it had the foresight to form an alliance with the rising power of Rome in the west, and that kept it safe for a time. However, in 30 B.C., it too was absorbed by the expansive Romans.

As we approach 1 B.C./A.D. 1, then, Greece, after a century as the intellectual light of the west, and another century in which its culture spread all over the civilized world, is merely a Roman province. It rests quietly among the glowing embers of a past that was the most glorious in the history of humanity so far.

As the Roman sun rises, not only Greece but also Egypt and all the important cultures of the past began to fade back into the shaded regions of history.

The Romans Rule

WHILE THE GREEKS WERE THE MORE INTELLECTUAL AND inventive of the two cultures, the Romans must also be given credit for creative political experimentation. They lived under kings as a republic, and they went a long way toward making the empire a viable political system. In the end, they failed to resolve the old civilization/tribal struggle, and the fall of Rome is seen even today as a terrible loss to the world.

Founding of Rome

According to tradition Rome was founded in 753 B.C. For several centuries, it was ruled by kings and dominated by the Etruscan culture to the north. The Etruscans reached the peak of their influence in 535 B.C., when, in alliance with Carthage, they defeated a fleet of Greek ships off the island of Corsica in the Battle of Alalia. This put an end to Greek colonization in the Mediterranean and was the first decisive sea battle in history.

After that, however, the Etruscan civilization weakened because Celtic tribes (Gauls) from north of the Alps began moving into Italy and putting pressure on the Etruscan cities. Rome seized this opportunity to break free of Etruscan domination and overthrow its monarcy in 509 B.C.

Rome set up a republic initially ruled by an oligarchy under two consuls, who were annually elected. The Romans thought that two leaders would be best because each would jealously prevent the other from growing too strong. Their chief function was to lead the armies, while the actual machinery of government remained in the hands of the Senate, consisting of members of the society's leading families (patricians).

The common people, known as plebians, resisted the oligarchy and the struggle between rich and poor became a dominant theme in Rome, as it had been in Greece. In response to the tensions between the two classes, the Romans showed their genius for creative government. Under similar circumstances, the Greek cities all too often engaged in civil wars or slipped into tyranny, but the Romans worked out compromises in which the plebians shared in the government enough to be satisfied.

The Romans were also a legalistic people, and by 450 B.C. they had written a law-code that did much to stabilize their society and remained a model to others through the ages. Rome also formed a Latin league of cities south of the Tiber River to counterbalance the Etruscan city-union north of the Tiber.

The Gauls had little interest in all these developments, and they did not halt their incursions at the Etruscan border. In 390 B.C., they actually occupied Rome, an event that crippled the city for a short time and traumatized its citizens for a much longer period. It was not until 350 B.C. that Rome even began to recover from this invasion.

One key to the Roman success was their development of the legion, a flexible fighting force much more adaptable to rough terrain than the phalanx had been. The legion could tighten itself into a phalanx, but it could also loosen up into a more open formation that flowed around obstacles.

Rome fought with the other cities in central Italy and usually won. Its use of the legion, together with its efficient system of government supported the making of wise decisions under pressure and led to many victories. By 290 B.C., Rome controlled central Italy, and its genius for government showed up again in how it ruled the defeated foes.

Rome generally allowed those it conquered to keep their old rulers and customs, and the Romans made enough concessions to prevent rebellions or quiet them once they began. Often, the conquered cities found that they were better off under Rome's efficient system of government than they had been by themselves.

A major advantage of Roman rule was that Rome kept the peace, while freedom often meant that the cities simply remained in perpetual war with one another.

Once Rome had securely fastened its grip on central Italy, the Greek cities to the south grew fearful. By that time, the Hellenistic kingdoms had been established, and the Greeks called on the nearest, Epirus, for aid. Epirus, just across the narrow strait from the Italian heel, was ruled by a general named Pyrrhus (319–272 B.C.). He arrived in southern Italy in 280 B.C. with his Macedonian phalanx and a number of war elephants (a military innovation first encountered by Alexander the Great, who was opposed in India by elephants used as "living tanks").

Rome destroys Carthage

The Romans were able to defeat Pyrrhus once they solved the problem of the elephants and the phalanx, after which they were confronted with the Carthaginians and Hannibal. After defeating the Carthaginians in a series of punishing and ruthless struggles, the Romans picked off the Hellenistic kingdoms one by one. Eventually, Roman rule seemed so inevitable that its opponents gave up without a fight. King Attalus III of the Hellenistic kingdom of Pergamum, for example, died without heirs in 133 B.C. He simply left his realm to Rome, on the grounds that they would take it anyway and he felt his action would at least avoid bloodshed.

Rome becomes leading power of Mediterranean

By 130 B.C., Rome had become the supreme power in the Mediterranean. There have been efforts to explain the early success of republican Rome, and it seems clear that many different factors worked together to support their rise to primacy.

As we have seen, innovations in military technology and strategy helped propel many societies to leadership, but it rarely kept them there. Thus, while the prowess of the Roman legion must be taken into account, we must look at other factors to explain Rome's dominance.

Their facility at road building certainly played a part. Rome built straight, wide, well-paved roads along which their armies could travel swiftly. Rome could shift forces from one region to another with smooth efficiency, which gave it a great advantage over its enemies. The roads were also highways for commerce, ordinary travel, and communications.

Rome's devotion to the law was also critical. The laws were worked out in great detail and applied to Romans and non-Romans alike. Legal opinions were binding and precedents were seen as important. In short, Roman law has been the foundation of European law, and to some extent, world law ever since. It was the law that kept the Roman realm stable, and made it acceptable to most of its people.

However, not everyone was satisfied with Roman rule. The wars flooded the Roman realm with slaves who were used on large plantations that squeezed out the small farmers. The wars and administration of conquered provinces created an influx of new wealth and profiteers, resulting in an ever-widening gap between rich and poor.

In 135 B.C., the first of the slave rebellions took place, breaking out in Sicily where the slaves were treated with especially cruel inhumanity. Rome managed to defeat the slave rebellions but the revolts were costly, and the upper classes always suffered serious casualties. The rebellions eventually died out, partly because the Romans realized that they would have to treat slaves more humanely and partly because the numbers of slaves declined as the Romans ran out of enemies to defeat.

Social unrest also troubled the empire at large. Certain liberal Roman politicians wanted to reform society to limit the amount of land and wealth that individuals could accumulate, and to work out a land reform to prevent the small farmers from becoming paupers. Two brothers, Tiberius Sempronius Gracchus (163–133 B.C.) and Gaius Sempronius Gracchus (153–121 B.C.), were outstanding leaders among the reformers. Both were assassinated by thugs hired by conservatives who benefited from the status quo and wanted it to continue.

This discord did not prevent the Roman realm from continuing to expand and take in parts of North Africa that had still been under native rule. Then, in 113 B.C. Rome was suddenly threatened by a new force—not from any civilized power but from the tribesmen of the north moving southward across Gaul, and toward Roman regions. The Romans, who had never forgotten the sack of Rome by the Gauls, panicked and turned to Gaius Marius (157–86 B.C.), who had been a conqueror in North Africa.

Marius raised an army of the poor and dispossessed and he completely wiped out the invading tribes in two battles. Rome was saved, but Marius had set a dangerous precedent that troubled Rome for many years after. His army was a personal army rather than a Roman one, and the soldiers owed allegiance to him, rather than to Rome in the abstract. Other generals took the same approach, and over half a century of civil wars followed.

The conflicts divided along class lines. Marius took the side of the poor. Lucius Cornelius Sulla (138–78 B.C.) opposed him, supporting the old ways. By 82 B.C., Sulla had won the civil war and tried to reestablish the old senatorial supremacy. However, after his death, the wars began again. New champions of the people appeared on the scene, most notable among them being Gaius Julius Caesar (100–44 B.C.).

Rome was an extraordinarily resilient society in those pre-Christian days, and the civil wars did not slow her expansion any more than slave rebellions and social turmoil had. For example, the kingdoms of Pontus and Armenia in Asia Minor tried to take advantage of the Roman divisions to free themselves. Pontus launched a surprise attack in 88 B.C., driving the Romans right out of Asia Minor. The Romans recovered and returned in force under the leadership of Pompeius (Pompey). They annexed Pontus and turned Armenia into a puppet kingdom, then annexed Syria and Judea.

Finally, Pompey, a popular leader because of his victories, united with Caesar, who had enormous charm and oratorical capabilities, and Crassus, the richest man in Rome. They formed a *triumvirate* (Latin for "three men"), yet another political experiment, and forced peace on Rome.

Once that was accomplished, each of the three took a province for himself. Caesar took Roman Gaul (consisting of northern Italy and what is now the coast of southern France), and Crassus took Syria. Pompey took Spain but preferred to stay in Italy where he would be close to the seat of power.

Crassus' mission proved to be disastrous. He intended to fight the Parthians and extend Roman power in that direction. He was, however, defeated and killed at the Battle of Carrhae in western Parthia.

Caesar, on the other hand, who had never before fought in a battle, found that he was a military genius at the age of forty-two. In the seven-year campaign he conquered all of Gaul and annexed it to the Roman realm. He even raided the island of Britain in 54 B.C. Like Alexander the Great, Caesar never lost a battle.

Pompey grew jealous of Caesar's victories and threw in his lot with the Senate and the conservatives against Caesar. When Caesar tried to return to Rome in 49 B.C., he was ordered to do so without his army. Knowing that if he complied he would be helpless before his enemies now that they had been joined again by Pompey, he defied orders and returned *with* his army—which meant civil war again.

The moment of truth came when Caesar crossed the Rubicon River into Roman territory in defiance of the Senate's orders. Crossing the Rubicon has ever since meant taking a step from which there is no retreat.

Pompey did not dare to face Caesar and his battle-hardened legions, and he fled to Greece. Most of the senators and many other conservatives went with him.

Caesar followed in 48 B.C., and the two Roman generals finally met in battle at Pharsalia in southern Thessaly. Caesar defeated Pompey, who fled to Egypt. He thought he would be safe there, because it was not Roman territory at the time. The Egyptians did not, however, want to run afoul of the increasingly powerful Caesar, and they killed Pompey as soon as he landed.

Caesar followed Pompey to Egypt, where he found the young and beautiful Egyptian queen Cleopatra VII (69–30 B.C.). Caesar remained with her for three months and then went to Asia Minor to fight at Pontus one last time. In Pontus he had a particularly easy victory and sent a message to Rome, which said, simply, *Veni, vidi, vici* ("I came, I saw, I conquered").

Caesar returned to Rome in 45 B.C. as its absolute master. He began the task of reform by increasing the number of senators, redistributing the land, widening Roman citizenship, and forcing the Romans to adopt a form of the Egyptian calendar (which is essentially the system that we use today).

Julius Caesar assassinated

The conservatives, whose predecessors had assassinated the Gracchus brothers, were not about to let Caesar have his way, powerful though he might be. Tradition tells us that on March 15, 44 B.C., a soothsayer approached Caesar as he left his home for the Senate and told him, "Beware the Ides of March." While the story of that encounter may be a legend, it is a historical fact that Caesar was assassinated that day by a group of conspirators under the leadership of Marcus Junius Brutus (85–42 B.C.) and Gaius Cassius Longinus (d. 42 B.C.).

The plotters had not made plans for capitalizing on their efforts, however, and Caesar's great popularity made for their undoing. Caesar's lieutenant Mark Antony used his funeral oration to rouse the crowds against Brutus and the others, and they were forced to flee from Rome.

In their absence, Caesar's great-nephew, the nineteen-year-old Gaius Octavianus (63 B.C.–A.D. 14) arrived in Rome. He and Mark Antony joined with the Roman general Marcus Aemilius Lepidus to form the second triumvirate. They followed the conspirators to Greece in 42 B.C. and defeated them at the Battle of Philippi in eastern Macedonia. Both Brutus and Cassius committed suicide after the battle had been lost.

The triumvirate then divided the empire among themselves. Octavian took the west, including Rome, the seat of political power. Mark Antony took the east, the source of the empire's wealth. Lepidus, the minor partner, took Africa.

Lepidus tried to extend his power to Sicily, but Octavian imprisoned his rival and took Africa from him. Octavian then reigned supreme in the west.

Now it was Mark Antony's turn to encounter Cleopatra, and, like Caesar, he fell in love with her. After being defeated by the Parthians in 36 B.C., he gave up war and politics and went to Alexandria to live a life of ease with the Egyptian queen.

Octavian turned Roman public opinion against Mark Antony by describing him as a slave of a foreign monarch and as planning to give half of the Roman realm to Egypt. War between Octavian and Antony became inevitable, and on September 2, 31 B.C., the greatest naval battle of ancient times was fought at Actium off the west coast of Greece. Octavian's fleet won under the leadership of an able general, Agrippa. Antony and Cleopatra fled to Egypt, and when Octavian pursued them they killed themselves.

The Roman civil wars had finally ended in dramatic fashion, and the truth was that the republic had died with them. Octavian was now the absolute ruler of Rome. He annexed Egypt as a personal possession, putting an end to the Hellenistic monarchies.

Octavian, without altering the form of the republic, managed to modify it so that he became the supreme authority, holding all the important posts. On January 23, 27 B.C., Octavian was named Augustus Caesar. He became the imperator, (or generalissimo of the armies) or emperor, in English. In 27 B.C., what had been the Roman Republic ended, and the Roman Empire came into being, with Augustus as the first emperor.

Octavian (Caesar Augustus) becomes emperor of Rome

In 1 B.C./A.D. 1, civilization had reached a new level in the Western world. All the civilized areas west of the Euphrates had been combined under Rome, and peace, known as the Pax Romana, extended over the entire region. The Roman Empire was certainly the most stable yet seen in the west, and it boasted a population of some 40 million people, twice that of Alexander's empire.

All seemed well under the beneficent rule of Augustus, but the Romans, as they would soon discover, had lost as much as they had gained by giving up their republican principles. Before the next millennium was half over, the Roman Empire would be no more.

India Becomes a Spiritual Center

NDIA, WHILE FIGHTING OFF THE INCURSIONS OF ALEXANDER the Great, also continued to distinguish itself as a birthplace for new religions. Perhaps uniquely, it also organized society around its spiritual values. During this period, the caste system was coming into existence, a reflection of the Hindu belief in reincarnation. It divided the population into a hierarchy of positions, depending on family, marriage, and occupation. In theory, you were born into a given caste in order to have the appropriate experiences in this lifetime and evolve spiritually.

In practice, the system gave everyone a secure place in society, which was stabilizing, but it also prevented anyone from advancing themselves. The system acted to inhibit change and enforced a social stagnation that troubles India even today.

India did offer more to the world than religious thought. Some time before 800 B.C., Indian mathematicians first began to use a symbol for zero, an intellectual advance of tremendous importance. This made it possible to tell the difference between 23, 203, and 230, and one didn't need special symbols for tens and hundreds. Positional notation now became possible, greatly simplifying arithmetical computation. However, the use of the zero idea spread rather slowly, so firm was the hold of the older and far less useful number-symbol systems.

Birth of Siddhartha Gautama (The Buddha) in India

By 500 B.C., many new religions were sprouting in the fertile soil of India, but none was more important on the world scene than Buddhism. Founded in northern India by Siddartha Gautama (563–483 B.C.) who came to be known as the Buddha ("enlightened one"), Buddhism did not have a God at its center. It stressed virtuous living, and preached the rebirth of the soul over and over until, through earned merit, the final reward of nirvana, or peaceful nonexistence, was attained.

Buddhism spread throughout eastern Asia, though it virtually died out in India itself. It represented India's greatest philosophic influence on the rest of the world.

In 321 B.C., the Indian chieftain Chandragupta began the process of unifying India. Under him a union of considerable portions of the peninsula occurred for the first time. He successfully held off the armies of Seleucus I in 305 B.C., as western forces, following the lead of Alexander, tried to exert control over India.

Chandragupta's dynasty reached its zenith under Asoka, who came to the throne in 265 B.C. He controlled all of India except the extreme southern portion. He easily could have conquered that area, as well, but instead he chose the road of Solomon rather than that of Caesar. Sickened by the slaughter of battle early in his career, he refused to fight anymore, and turned instead to the task of bettering his realm. India, under Asoka, may have reached a population of 30 million, considerably more than that of the Hellenistic kingdoms of that time. Again, however, the success of the kingdom was tied to the king, and the empire disintegrated after Asoka's death in 236 B.C..

By 1 B.C./A.D. 1, India was once again in a state of fragmentation and had lost its ability to influence the rest of the world, except philosophically.

C HINA REMAINED DIVIDED INTO FEUDAL KINGDOMS IN THE *China Follows* first part of this millennium, but by 600 B.C. it had also *Its Own Path* entered the Iron Age.

In a major development, schools of ethics began to appear in China at this time. One, supposedly founded by the legendary Lao-Tzu, started around 565 B.C. His philosophy is called Taoism, and it eschewed all form, ritual, and ceremony. It taught that following the Tao, or way, coupled with right living, was most important.

The influence of Taoism has been felt primarily in how it has affected other more structured religious systems. For example, Taoism is a strong current in Zen Buddhism.

Around 500 B.C., Kung Fu-tzu (551–479 B.C.), or Confucius, taught a highly developed system of morality and ethical behavior that was quite different from Taoism. Confucius' codes became institutionalized and permeated the society and governmental system of China.

In 221 B.C., China was finally unified under the Ch'in dynasty. The first emperor of China was Shih Huang Ti (259–210 B.C.), and in his time he may have ruled over as many as 30 million people.

Shih was anxious to wipe out traces of the long feudal past and to begin history anew. For this reason, he ordered all books to be destoryed except scientific works, which remained in the hands of offical scholars. While his desire to free China from the past may have been laudable, his actions certainly impoverished the knowledge of future generations about that period in his nation's history.

He also supervised the building of an earthen mound across the northern border of the country. This barrier became known as the Great Wall of China, and it served as a barrier against the nomadic tribes to the north. It was not intended so much to keep out people, but their horses. Tribesmen without their horses were far less dangerous warriors, in the eyes of the Chinese.

The Ch'in dynasty's rule was short. In 202 B.C., the Han dynasty replaced it and managed to keep China united.

Under the Han dynasty in 110 B.C., the Chinese, under Emperor Wu Ti, advanced south of the Yangtze River and annexed all of what is now southern China. In 108 B.C., they conquered Korea. Wherever Chinese armies fought, Chinese culture followed, much as Greek culture had spread throughout the Western world.

China developed in almost total isolation from the west until a Chinese explorer named Chang Ch'ien (d. 114 B.C.) traveled to Bactria (in what is now Afghanistan) to obtain help against the Huns. This was the first known contact between China and the west, and it had profound effects by fueling the western appetites for silk and other goods.

Thus, in B.C./A.D. 1, there was a Chinese empire just about as large and powerful as the Roman Empire, but the two knew very little about each other.

T HE WORLD POPULATION, WHICH HAD BEEN ABOUT 50 million in 1000 B.C., had more than tripled in the following millennium, becoming 170 million at 1 B.C./A.D. 1. Of these, there were about 40 million in the Roman Empire, 30 million in China, 30 million in India, 5 million in Parthia, and 65 million scattered over the rest of the world.

The World Moves Ahead

World population at 170 million

In only a few millennia, humans had invented several new political systems, including democracy, the republic, and the empire. Democracy seems to have taken hold only in Greece, and the Romans abandoned their experiment with republican government to embrace the imperial form.

The empire seemed to dominate as the time of Chirst approached, even though it was always an unpredictable solution. It was made possible by many other inventions, such as writing and roads, that allowed rulers to control large regions of territory, such as writing and roads. During this era, the empire replaced the city-state as the primary approach to organizing society.

Civilization had advanced everywhere, but the great civilizations often remained separate from one another. The relative stability of the civilized areas supported the rapid growth of population, which in turn drove human inventiveness to new heights as people struggled to provide for increasingly larger societies.

To those living in the great empires of the time, it may have seemed that life would go on in that way forever. The Romans in particular may have believed that the Eternal City would live up to its name.

However, major changes that would shake the world were on the horizon as this millennium drew to a close.

CHAPTER FIVE

THE FIRST REAL MILLENNIUM

(A.D. 1000)

(*Author's Note*: As we move into the Christian era, we will no longer need to continue distinguishing B.C. from A.D. so often. When a number appears, unadorned, [as 123, for example] it should be read as A.D.)

D URING ALL THE MILLENNIA THAT HAVE BEEN DISCUSSED SO far, very few people thought in terms of thousand-year periods. As we have already noted, counting time from the birth of Jesus did not originate until late in this millennium. Moreover, millennial thinking, or ascribing great significance to the end and beginning of millennia, did not begin until the very end of this millennium. Because of certain passages in the biblical Book of Revelation, some people believed that the end of the world would occur in the year A.D. 1000.

Thus, the time from 1 B.C./A.D. 1 to A.D. 1000 can be called the first real millennium, in that it was the first time that there was a consciousness of thousand-year periods. At the beginning of this period, the rule of Rome permeated much of the world. By the end, Rome had become the center for a new kind of empire, one that rested on spiritual rather than material values. Elsewhere, great changes also took place as the foundation was laid for our own millennium and modern times.

Rome Falls

THE ROMAN REPUBLIC HAD BEEN AN EXPANSIONIST STATE since its founding. Once it had been converted to an empire, the impetus to expand was increased, rather than reduced. The Parthians had stopped Rome at Carrhae in 53 B.C., but battles in the east continued. The Roman Empire also absorbed areas on its own boundaries, and they became Roman puppets while retaining their own rulers.

The Atlantic Ocean bounded Rome on the west, the Sahara Desert on the south, the Parthian frontier on the east, and the course of the Rhine and Danube rivers on the north. The major expansionist effort was made to the north where Roman armies advanced from the Rhine to the Elbe rivers, attempting to include the German tribes within the empire.

Roman defeat in Teutoberg Forest puts Empire on defensive

However, the Roman thrust into this region brought disaster instead. Three Roman legions were trapped and annihilated in the Teutoberg Forest in the year 9. This great loss broke Augustus's will and diminished his thirst for continued growth. He withdrew behind the Rhine and from then on, the Roman Empire remained almost entirely on the defensive.

There were always exceptions, of course. In 43, when Claudius (10 B.C.–A.D. 54) was emperor, the legions took the southern portion of the island of Britain and made it into a Roman province. A half century later, Emperor Trajan (53–117) attacked and absorbed Dacia, north of the Danube (modern Romania). Between 113 and 117, he finally defeated the Parthians and annexed the Tigris-Euphrates Valley.

At that moment, the Roman legions stood at the Persian Gulf and the empire was at its fullest extent, its population totaling as much as 50 million.

However, Trajan's successor Hadrian (76–138) abandoned the Parthian conquests and built a wall across Britain's narrowest point. His act was a message that there would be no attempt to extend the realm there, and that the empire would merely defend itself against the onslaughts of the Picts, living in what is now Scotland.

Even if the Roman Empire was no longer keen on foreign adventures, it did bring the Mediterranean world a two-century-long period of peace after its founding. As already noted, this time is called the Pax Romana (the Roman peace), and the civilized Western world had never seen such a period before or since (at least so far).

Just as several factors had combined to bring Pax Romana into being, a number of events helped bring it to a close. As in the past, the pressure of tribal peoples constantly threatened the empire and drained its resources. As in the case of Athens, uncontrolled illness not only checked Rome's population growth, but almost put it into decline. Then, too, the imperial system bred political instability because it provided no method for choosing a successor to the emperor, and no method of putting the brakes on emperors whose policies were irrational.

Finally, the impact of Christianity itself should not be under-emphasized. The new religion was alien to the Roman culture and essentially subversive in that its followers explicitly rejected the emperor as their highest authority.

The tribal problem began to appear insoluble during the early centuries of this millennium. Whereas Julius Caesar had entered the Gauls' territories and put the pressure on them, later emperors were forced onto the defensive, focusing on keeping the tribes out of Roman lands.

The tribes in Germany and to the east were increasingly hostile, and they pushed against the northern Roman borders, as tribes in central Asia moved westward against them.

Central Asia had always served as a reservoir for restless nomads. In times of reasonable pasture, the tribal population increased, and when the land became more arid, they could no longer be supported and pushed south and west to survive.

These Asian tribesmen sometimes reached Europe, pushing the European tribes ahead of them. In this way, the civilized Mediterranean areas suffered the depradations of the Cimmerians, Scythians, Gauls, and other Celts. Now it was the Germans who were spreading southward and eastward from their original Scandinavian homeland until they stood all along the Rhine and Danube borders.

In 166, when Marcus Aurelius (121–180) was emperor, a German tribe called the Marcomanni crossed the upper Danube, and the Romans had to fight them continually for some fifteen years. This conflict was the beginning of the barbarian invasions, which continued sporadically thereafter. While these invasions were fought off for two centuries, it was done with increasing effort and escalating costs.

Even as the Marcomanni invaded, a terrible plague was brought back into the empire by soldiers who had been fighting in the east. It seriously depopulated and weakened the empire, which never quite recovered.

In addition, the empire still had not established a clear method for choosing a successor when an emperor died. Since the army was the strongest force in the empire, the succession turned into an elective procedure in which the legions did the choosing. As early as 69, on the death of Nero (37–68), different candidates served as emperor for short periods until the army was able to put Vespasian (9–79) on the throne. The situation deteriorated after the death of Marcus Aurelius. For a century, emperors came and went rapidly at the whim of the military.

The empire also failed to develop an appropriate method of taxation, so that its economy declined, and the loyalty of the population to the government and the state decreased almost to the vanishing point.

These were systemic problems that could not be solved without radical changes in the nature of the society. Various emperors did try to institute reforms and arrest the steady decline of the empire, but to no avail.

For example, Diocletian (245–305) divided the empire into four regions to make it more governable. He also abandoned the pretense that the old republic was still in force, and converted the empire into an absolute monarchy. His efforts only served to weaken the system, however, because the rulers of the four regions now began to fight one another.

Constantine I (288–337) became emperor in 306 and made perhaps the most fundamental change in the empire to that time. He moved the imperial capital from Rome to Byzantium (renamed Constantinople in his honor) on the Bosporus. The new capital was in a strong position, and the eastern portion of the empire became richer and more civilized than the west, but the move weakened the western provinces.

Constantine I becomes Roman Emperor; "Christianizes" the Empire

During all this time, the German tribes remained a serious threat and became an even greater danger when the Huns of central Asia started pushing westward. Suddenly, the German Goths found themselves the hunted rather than the hunters, and they had no choice but to push harder against the gates of the empire.

In 376, tribes known as the Visigoths crossed the Danube into the Balkan peninsula. They came as refugees rather than as raiders but were badly mistreated by Roman officials. As a result, they took up arms against the empire.

On August 9, 378, the Battle of Adrianople was fought. The Goths won because they capitalized on a simple but highly effective development in military technology. They had picked up the use of stirrups, which had been invented some time before in central Asia. Stirrups enabled horsemen to keep their seats when their spears struck the enemy. This brought the united weight of man and horse to bear upon the objective and made the cavalry enormously more effective.

The Gothic cavalry wiped out the Roman legions, and seven centuries of Roman prowess in battle abruptly ended. From now on, it was the cavalry that ruled the battlefield.

The Romans did manage to recover from their defeat, and under Theodosius I (346–395) the empire was united for the last time. After his death, it was once again divided—this time between his two sons—and never united again. Arcadius (377–408) ruled the East Roman Empire from Constantinople; Honorius (384–423) ruled the West Roman Empire from Milan, and later from Ravenna. Both sons proved to be incompetent rulers, and the Roman armies had to turn to the Germans for leadership and rank and file soldiers.

Rome sacked by Visigoths

By now, the empire was little more than a pale reflection of what it once had been. Beginning in 406, the German tribes broke into Gaul and the Roman armies were unable to drive them out. Britain was abandoned by the Romans in 407, and in 410 the city of Rome itself was sacked by the Visigoths under the leadership of Alaric (370–410). This attack came exactly eight hundred years after the original sack of Rome by the Gauls.

The West Roman Empire began to disintegrate as the German tribes started setting up kingdoms in the Roman provinces. The Visigoths carved out their kingdom in southwestern Gaul and in Spain. Another tribe, the Vandals, took over the north African provinces. The Huns moved westward on their heels and under their king Attila (406–453) formed a large but thinly held empire, stretching from the Caspian Sea nearly to the Atlantic.

Attila the Hun defeated

In the center of Gaul, a Roman-Gothic army under Aetius managed to defeat Attila at the Battle of Chalons in June, 451. Attila died two years later, and the Hunnic Empire disintegrated almost at once. The immediate threat from the Huns had been dissipated, but the damage had already been done.

Fall of Roman Empire in the West; Dark Age begins in Europe

The West Roman Empire continued to disintegrate, and nothing could be done now to stop it. In 476, the last Roman emperor with his capital in Italy, Romulus Augustulus, was deposed, with no successor at hand. It is this moment in history that is usually described as the fall of the Roman Empire. However, that is a reflection of our narrow view, because only the West Roman Empire really fell. The East Roman Empire actually remained strong and intact. Nevertheless, it was an event of great importance, heralding the onset of a difficult time, and proving once again that the forward march of civilization was not an inevitable process.

The Dark Ages Descend

ITALY NOW CAME UNDER THE RULE OF THE GERMANIC TRIBES and in 489 was taken over by the Ostrogoths under King Theodoric (454–526). Britain was then invaded by Germanic tribes, the Angles, Saxons, and Jutes. In 481, Gaul was also invaded by a new Germanic tribe, the Franks, under King Clovis (466–511).

By 500, all vestiges of the West Roman Empire had virtually disappeared. The political situation had reversed itself, as all the provinces were now under tribal rule, with a new Germanic aristocracy lording it over a lower class descended from the old Romans.

In terms of social evolution, it might well have been necessary for the political grip of the empire to be loosened, so that a new and more vital society could take its place. The real loss was that of all the knowledge of Greek learning in the west, and the strength of civilization's institutions, such as the rule of law.

The process had been seen before, however, in Sumeria, for example. As Roman cities, roads, and institutions deteriorated and fell apart, western Europe entered a dark age. Looking back on it with our western viewpoint, we tend to think of this dark age as worldwide, but it was not. It included only the western provinces of what had been the Roman Empire. The East Roman Empire and many of the Asian kingdoms were doing quite well, and their civilizations functioned at a high level.

It was from the east, in fact, that civilization was eventually reestablished in western Europe. In the east, the legacy of Greek learning and culture was preserved, and this kept the flame of knowledge burning for several hundred years, while the west struggled to find a new path.

Most of the Germanic kingdoms did not last very long. The Vandals in northern Africa were destroyed by the East Roman Empire in 534, and the Ostrogoths met the same fate in 544. The Lombards, another Germanic tribe, moved into the power vacuum, however, preventing the reestablishment of Roman rule.

The Visigoths in Spain were overcome by invaders from North Africa. These invaders were from a region called Mauritania, and the Spaniards called them Moros. We call them Moors, and they proved to be a problem for the Europeans throughout the Dark Ages.

The Franks were the only Germanic kingdom that really flourished. Unfortunately, they were the least civilized of all the tribes that had dismantled the Roman Empire, and their reign delayed recovery from the Dark Ages. (The Roman province of Gaul eventually came to be called France because it was ruled by the Franks.)

The Franks had the unfortunate habit of dividing the kingdom among their sons, so that their realms were forever being fragmented and the sons were forever fighting one another. These perpetual civil wars served to deepen the Dark Ages still further.

There were occasional hopeful signs. For example, the descendants of Clovis, the founder of the Frankish kingdom, were called the Merovingians, from a reputed ancestor of Clovis. They brought some light into the darkness with relatively successful reigns, but they gradually declined in ability, and the last strong Merovingian ruling all the Franks was Dagobert I (605–639).

Charles Martel defeats Moors at Battle of Tours

After his death, the rulership was taken over by a line of ministers who served under a series of do-nothing kings. Charles Martel (688–741), meaning Charles the Hammer, was a prominent minister in this line, and he did manage to do some things well. He took on the responsibility of confronting the Moors, who had taken over Spain and were threatening the rest of Europe. Martel developed heavy cavalry, using large horses strong enough to carry armor and a rider encased in armor. With these new versions of the living tank, he met the Moors in the Battle of Tours in central France.

The Moors were unable to counter this innovation in military strategy, and they were defeated soundly. Eventually, they were forced to retreat beyond the Pyrenees, providing Europe with a reasonable opportunity to recover from its difficulties.

Charles Martel's son, Pepin the Short (714–768), took over the ministry of the Frankish kingdom on his father's death. He was not content to be merely a minister, and in 751 he deposed the last Merovingian monarch and became a king himself, founding the Carolingian dynasty.

Then, his son Charles (742–814) succeeded to the throne in 768, and was so successful that he became known as Charles the Great, or, in French, Charlemagne. Charlemagne aggressively attempted to expand his kingdom, striking first at the Moors and taking over a strip of land south of the Pyrenees known as the Spanish March. He also destroyed the Lombard kingdom in Italy and made most of it part of his realm. He moved eastward against the Saxons and extended his new empire in that direction.

In 800, Charlemagne had himself crowned emperor, making for a kind of restoration of the West Roman Empire, although the East Roman Empire refused to recognize the validity of that restoration.

Charlemagne crowned Emperor

Charlemagne's Frankish Empire included the nations we now know as France, the Netherlands, Belgium, western Germany, most of Italy, and parts of Spain. Of the various provinces of the West Roman Empire, North Africa, and Spain were still controlled by the Moors, and Saxon Britain (now called England) remained under rulers of its own. However, all the rest was now Frankish, together with some eastern areas that had never been part of the Roman Empire.

It was not the Pax Romana, but within the Frankish Empire, Charlemagne did keep the peace, and tried to bring back elements of civilization. Population in areas such as Gaul, which had been declining, began to rise again, and Charlemagne reestablished schools and encouraged education. He worked hard to lighten the Dark Ages just a bit.

Unfortunately, the success of Charlemagne's empire did not last beyond his death. His only son and successor Louis the Pious (778–840) was a weak ruler. Louis himself had several sons, and he continued the tradition of dividing the realm among them. The result was civil war both during his lifetime and after his death. The Dark Ages closed in on Europe once again.

Charlemagne's empire broke up permanently in 843, with the signing of the Treaty of Verdun among Louis' sons. East and west now parted company—even their languages had become quite different. The east became what is now Germany, and the west became what is now France.

New waves of tribal invasions hastened the disintegration of the Frankish Empire. At the time, Scandinavia was experiencing a population increase that its frigid climate could not support.

Bands of Vikings therefore moved outward by land or sea to find loot and new homes.

Swedish bands invaded the land we now call Russia. Norwegian and Danish sea-raiders looted the sea coasts of the British Isles, and the Frankish Empire. They even penetrated into the Mediterranean Sea.

New Invaders from the east had arrived as well. The Alans had set up an eastern empire in Charlemagne's time, and, since then, tribes of Bulgars were ravaging the east. In the Mediterranean, African raiders took over the islands of Sicily, Sardinia, and the Balearics.

The rulers of these lands were helpless, and the common people gathered in terror around local nobles who could offer some resistance. Thus, the incompetent Frankish king, Charles III (879–929), who came to the throne in 893, coped with the last Norse invasion in 911 by granting them a province at the mouth of the Seine to make their own. In this way, the Duchy of Normandy was founded. His action contrasted sharply with that of Odo, Count of Paris, who withstood a Viking raid on Paris in 885 and drove the attackers away.

It is not surprising that the Franks eventually abandoned the failing Carolingian line. The last Carolingian to rule the eastern Franks, or Germans, was Louis III (893–911). When he died, there were no Carolinigian successors and the Germans now chose a ruler from among their nobility.

The last Carolingian to rule the west Franks, or French, was Lothair, who died in 986. He was succeeded by Hugh Capet, the great-grandson of Count Odo.

Neither France nor Germany under their new kings was a strong, unified monarchy. The disorganizations of the Carolingian civil wars and of the Viking raids had increased the power of the nobility and weakened the central government. What had been the Frankish Empire, particularly the French part, was now a collection of provinces whose rulers were virtually independent of the central monarchy.

Each province now went its own way, and fought with its neighbors; western Europe had become almost completely feudal.

The imperial crown, passed on by Charlemagne to descendants of lesser capability, had come to have virtually no significance at this time.

In 936, however, Germany came under the rule of Otto I (912– 973), the strongest king since Charlemagne, and he decided to revive the imperial idea. He began by subduing local rulers of Germany, then defeated invading tribes of Magyars from the east. He invaded Italy twice and finally forced his crowning as emperor in 962.

Otto I rules Holy Roman Empire

This period marked a true revival of the Roman Empire in the west. Of course, it was scarcely Roman, since the new emperor ruled only over Germany and northern Italy. To distinguish it from the old empire, which was larger and had been pagan for a long time, the new empire was called the Holy Roman Empire.

Otto III, the twenty-two-year-old grandson of Otto I, reigned over the Holy Roman Empire in 1000. He was married to a princess of the East Roman Empire, or Byzantine Empire, and his court was therefore subjected to the more civilized influences of the east.

Meanwhile, the thirty-year-old Robert II, a son of Hugh Capet, reigned over France. Feudalistic tendencies kept Robert II from being a strong king. Richard II, Duke of Normandy, was, for example, more powerful than the king.

Anglo-Saxon England had suffered greatly from Danish raids on its coasts, but was beginning slowly to recover. England had a capable king in Alfred (849–899), who had come to the throne in 871. Unfortunately, his successors did not live up to his example. In 1000, the English were ruled by Ethelred the Ill-Advised, whose name alone should indicate his level of success. He was forced to buy off the Danes rather than drive them away, and he did that job badly as well.

By 1000, then, western Europe was still in the throes of feudalism, but the Dark Ages were beginning to lift. As in the past, technological innovation played a major role in catalyzing social changes. Apparently simple inventions made a great difference. For example, the horse collar and horseshoes made it possible to use horses to pull plows. A new kind of moldboard plow was then developed that was far more efficient in turning over the damp, heavy soil of northwestern Europe.

These inventions led to an increase in the food supply in western Europe, and by the end of this millennium, the population of the area had returned to its level at the height of the Roman Empire—about 6.5 million in France and as much as 8 million in the entire Holy Roman Empire.

As we have seen since the beginning of our survey in the epoch before civilization, human inventiveness continued to drive human progress along, in spite of enormous hardships, deprivations, and poor political leadership. This was as true in A.D. 1000 as it had been in 8000 B.C.

The East Holds On

WHEN THE WEST ROMAN EMPIRE COLLAPSED IN 476, THE East Roman Empire survived. Indeed, the emperor, sitting in Constantinople, considered himself to have inherited all the western provinces.

The East Roman Empire had a problem, however, when it came to taking back the lost provinces by force. There continued to be no clear system for the succession of emperors so that dynastic quarreling and military interference went on without interruption. This kept the eastern Empire in turmoil, as did outside perils. To the east, the Parthian Empire had given way to a new Persian Empire, and it continued its centuries-long feud with the Romans. In addition, new waves of tribal invaders kept crossing the Danube and invading the Balkans.

The East Roman Empire had an experienced army that was able to fight off the invaders, and the fortified outposts of the empire, including Constantinople itself, held out. Constantinople was surrounded by strong walls and its sea approach was held by the East Roman navy, so it could neither be stormed nor starved out. Nevertheless, the constant fighting ravaged the East Roman land, killed its soldiers, and emptied it treasury.

In 527, a strong emperor, Justinian (483–565), came to the throne. He was determined to reconquer the west and he had a general of genius to realize his purpose—Belisarius. In 533,

Belisarius, commanding a small force, wiped out the Vandal kingdom in North Africa and reannexed it.

The former capital of the Vandal lands was Carthage, which had been rebuilt as a Roman city centuries after its destruction as a Phoenician city, and it now became an important Roman center again.

Belisarius then went on to re-take Italy from the Ostrogoths. This was a much more difficult job that took twenty years. In fact, it was only completed by Belisarius' successor, Narses, a general and administrator of genius who was over seventy when he took command. In 554, East Roman forces also took over sections of the Spanish coast. All this was done while there was still considerable fighting with the Persians in the east and the tribal invaders in the north.

However exciting and heroic the reconquest might have seemed, it did no good and strained the East Roman strength badly. The newly recovered provinces could not be held for very long and soon were lost to the Visigoths and other invaders. The East Romans managed to hold the south and a strip of the Italian midsection for some time. The primary result of the long fighting between the Ostrogoths and East Romans in Italy was to ruin that land and ensure that it entered into the Dark Ages, as had the Frankish kingdom. Only the African province remained as a relatively long-term adjunct to the East Roman Empire.

Justinian did better with his internal policies. He completely reformed the East Roman government, making it possible for the system to last longer than it otherwise would have. He collected and reorganized the Roman law, which had been accumulating precedents for centuries, thus establishing the Justinian Code, which served as a legal guide for all of Europe in the centuries to come.

Justinian also beautified Constantinople, which had been al-most destroyed by riots that had taken place in the early years of his reign. In particular, he built the Church of Hagia Sophia (Holy Wisdom), completing it in 537 with a large dome so cleverly pierced by windows that the entire interior was flooded with light. The dome itself looked as though it were floating on air.

It was easily predictable, however, that after Justinian's death, quarrels over the succession would again lead to chaos. While Constantinople continued to be burdened with endless dynastic struggles, Persia took the opportunity to make a sudden advance. At the time, Persia had a population of only 6 million, compared with the 14 million in the East Roman Empire. However, Persia was the more compact nation, while the East Romans were convulsed by civil war within and tribal invasion without.

Beginning in 606, Persia began stripping province after province from the East Roman Empire. By 619, they had even taken Asia Minor and Egypt. It appeared that Persia had almost reconstituted the ancient Persian Empire as it had been under Darius eleven centuries before. It also seemed that the East Roman Empire might be lost. The Visigoths had taken the Spanish coast and the Avars were at the walls of Constantinople.

In 610, Heraclius became emperor and undertook the thankless task of trying to rally the East Romans. While Persia went from victory to victory, he worked to reorganize and revitalize his army. In 622, he was ready, and using his navy he bypassed Asia Minor and landed troops at the eastern edge of the Black Sea. There, like Alexander the Great, he struck at Persia's heart. In three campaigns he defeated them, and by 630 all the lost territory had been re-taken.

The spectacular quarter-century war, however, had succeeded in ruining both protagonists. In 634, an army from Arabia, a region that had hitherto played little role in history, pushed northward and took on both Persia and the East Roman Empire, defeating the two exhausted nations with surprising speed. Next, the East Roman Empire lost Syria in 636, Judea in 637, Egypt in 640, and finally even Carthage in 698.

These losses were permanent. After this time, the area ruled from Constantinople is no longer called the East Roman Empire, but has become the Byzantine Empire to historians, or sometimes the Greek Empire. From this point on, however, Constantinople ruled over nothing more than Asia Minor and the Balkan peninsula. Its people were Greek speaking, but the emperors spoke of themselves as Roman emperors and their land as Rome until the very end.

The Arabs attacked Constantinople itself in 673, and for five years attempted to make a landing in the city. The Byzantine navy held them off with the help of a new invention that was called Greek fire. It contained naphtha and lime and other ingredients that made it a potent weapon. When the mixture was pushed out into the sea, the lime reacted with the water to develop heat that set the naphtha on fire.

If the flames reached the enemy's wooden ships, they were doomed. The sight of the fire burning on the water and the fear that it invoked was finally enough to drive off the Arabs. The Arabs tried again in 717, but they were driven off by an energetic emperor, Leo III, who used Greek fire as his primary weapon.

If the Arabs had taken Constantinople, there was little to the west that could have stopped them from further conquests. They could have raided into the eastern boundaries of the Frankish realm while the Moors in Spain were attacking the western boundaries. All of Europe might have fallen to the Arabs and the Moors, giving the region a distinctly different history than the one with which we are now familiar.

Constantinople held on, but then the Bulgars became a menace in the Balkans and the Byzantines had to fight them while also securing their boundaries against the Arabs in the east and south.

For two centuries after that, the Byzantine Empire continued to confront the Bulgarians, who together with the Slavs, occupied many of the Balkan regions permanently. As a result, the Balkan nations north of Greece today speak Slavic languages, except for Romania, which clings to a Latin-derived language. Though the Bulgars were of Asian descent, they intermarried with the Slavs and came to speak a Slavic dialect.

In 963, Basil II (958–1025) succeeded to the imperial throne. He was a child at the time, but the Byzantine Empire had two excellent generals, Nicephoras Phocas and John Tzimisces, to help him. They reconquered the island of Cyprus and extended the emperor's control over eastern Asia Minor and even into northern Syria.

When Basil grew old enough to rule on his own, he proved to

be a monarch interested only in war and spent fifty years engaged in fighting. He inflicted devastating defeats on the Bulgarians and brought the entire Balkan peninsula under Byzantine control.

Byzantine (East Roman) Empire at its peak

By the year 1000, the Byzantine Empire had reached its zenith. It was still only a fragment of what the Roman Empire had been at its peak, but it was by far the strongest power in Europe. Its population was at least 11 million, larger than any nation in western Europe, and its military machine was much more effective.

What's more, Constantinople had become the largest and richest city in Europe, perhaps in the world. It might have housed as many as 1 million inhabitants at this time. Whereas culture had sunk to a low ebb in the west, which was still climbing out of the Dark Ages, Constantinople was still the repository of all the learning of the Greeks. It boasted a large university and gifted scholars and was far more civilized than the primitive towns in the west.

Christianity's Influence Grows

IN THE TIME OF THE ROMAN EMPEROR AUGUSTUS, THE JEWS of Judea expectantly awaited a Messiah, and there were many candidates for the post. One of these was Jesus of Nazareth, whose life is described in the Gospels of the New Testament. The Jews were expecting a person who would not only lead them spiritually but also politically, liberating them from Roman rule. It was for this reason that descent from David loomed so large in determining who might be the Messiah, since he had been a successful king and empire builder.

As a result, both the Romans and some of the Jewish leaders of the time found the messianic fervor of the people threatening. According to the Bible, Jesus' influence increased rapidly, and many people began to follow him. When he came to Jerusalem with his disciples for Passover, there was great concern that he was about to lead another insurrection against Rome. Accordingly, he was seized, given a trial, and crucified for sedition, a typical Roman punishment for criminal activity.

For those who had believed in Jesus, it was a humiliating end to his ministry. It might well have been the end of his role, as it was for other reputed Messiahs of the time, but a remarkable man named Saul of Tarsus (d. about 65) became a follower of Jesus and transformed Christianity in the process.

Saul had been a persecutor of the early Christians, working on behalf of the Jewish authorities. However, he had a conversion experience on the road to Damascus, changed his name to Paul, and became the principal advocate of the new religion. By his preaching, the followers of Jesus (Messianists, or in Greek, Christians) became far more than just another Jewish sect. Paul abandoned strict adherence to the special rites of Judaism, such as dietary laws and circumcision, and separated Christianity from Judaism's national aspects. He began to convert Gentiles, who then became Christians without having to become Jews.

Some Jews also became Christians, but not very many did so. Most Jews were still waiting for a victorious military/political Messiah, not one who allowed himself to be crucified. By 66, they had grown tried of waiting, and rose in revolt against Rome. The results were catastrophic. The Jews fought ferociously and forced Rome to extend itself for many years, but in 70, Jerusalem was taken and the temple destroyed again—permanently, this time.

Jews' revolt against Rome is crushed; Temple destroyed

The last remnants of this revolt were crushed in 73. However, the Jews never accepted Roman rule, and they revolted again from 132 to 135. This revolt led to Judea being emptied of Jews. From then until modern times, Jews existed only as scattered remnants among the nations of the world. This was the period of the *Diaspora*, a Greek word meaning "dispersion," and the wonder of it is that under these difficult circumstances, the Jews managed to retain their national and religious identity.

Jewish "Diaspora" begins

The Jewish Christians remained neutral during the rebellion. In the face of the Jewish hostility that followed, they more or less died out, and Christianity became an almost entirely Gentile religion.

Christianity flourished particularly in the Greek east, but had a strong presence in the western empire as well. Wherever it existed, the new religion periodically suffered from persecution because Christians would refuse to participate in the national religious rites. Christianity also split into numerous sects that disagreed with each other on various doctrinal points, and they argued with each other fiercely.

Despite persecution and internal quarreling, Christianity grew stronger and by the time of Constantine, Christians made up a cohesive and vigorous 10 percent of the Roman population. Constantine concluded that they could represent valuable support for him in his early struggles with other would-be emperors. In 313, he therefore declared himself in favor of religious toleration. By the end of his reign, he had been baptized and the empire officially became Christian, a complete reversal of Nero's policy, which had put countless Christians to death in the Coliseum.

Christians had fought for religious toleration when they were a persecuted minority but dropped that stance immediately when their faith became an official religion. In addition, Christianity continued to split into sects, resulting in an ongoing struggle among these groups for primacy.

In the early days of the Christian Empire, a group called Arians grew particularly strong. Arian missionaries converted the Germanic tribes and when those tribes set up kingdoms in the west, they became an Arian aristocracy, ruling over a Catholic populace. Ultimately, however, the Arians were converted back to the dominant doctrines.

As might be expected, the chief rivalry within the church came to be that between the two great capitals of the empire: Rome, the old capital, and Constantinople, the new one. Both the bishop of Rome and the patriarch of Constantinople claimed to be the true head of the church.

One might have supposed the patriarch of the rich and vigorous Constantinople would surely have won out over the bishop of a decaying Rome. However, in the east, sectarian rivalries had become very strong, and regions such as Egypt and Syria differed so entirely from Constantinople's doctrine that there was no chance they would accept the patriarch as leader. Also, strong emperors periodically ruled in Constantinople and they tended to dominate the patriarch, lessening his authority in the eyes of Christians. Finally, the rival religion of Islam tore away Syria, Egypt, and northern Africa from the rule of Constantinople.

By contrast, the bishop of Rome was unrivaled in the west.

There were long periods in which there was no emperor, or one who was weak or far away from the city. The occasional strong bishop of Rome, now called the pope, could exert a powerful influence. Thus, Pope Leo I (400–461) had the courage to face Attila the Hun in 452, at a time when there was no secular authority with the ability to do so. This act of courage won great prestige for the papacy. Gregory I (540–604) became pope in 590, and he established the papacy as it has existed afterward, firmly resisting all the novel doctrines that arose in the east.

Gregory I establishes modern Papacy

Over the years, the papacy waxed and waned in its power and influence, as secular institutions have always done. During the 900s there was a decline, but when Otto I revived the Holy Roman Empire in 962, the papacy recovered as well.

Meanwhile, although Christian provinces had been lost in Asia and Africa, Christianity was spreading northward. Just as Rome had been an expansionist power politically from its founding days, so was Christianity a missionary-oriented religion from the beginning. The Gospels tell of Jesus himself sending out his disciples to spread the good news of his message; the popes and patriarchs also supported this type of activity.

The popes encouraged the conversion of the pagans of Britain and Germany to Christianity of the western style. Meanwhile, the patriarchs supported missions to convert the pagans among the Balkan tribes to Christianity of the eastern type.

By 990, Constantinople had converted the Russian tribes to their brand of Christianity, a development of the greatest importance, given the influence that Russia has come to have over the world in general.

By the year 1000, then, Christianity, which had begun in Judea and spread quickly to Syria and Egypt, had forever lost those provinces and was confined primarily to Europe. There were now two rival types of Christianity, differing considerably in points of doctrine. The western variety Roman Catholic existed in western Europe—the Holy Roman Empire, France and Britain, for the most part. The eastern variety Greek Orthodox existed in Asia Minor, and the Balkans, and was just coming into existence in the region north of the Black Sea.

Overall, Christianity was still a minor religion, if the world is viewed as a whole. Islam seemed far more powerful and assertive, and the eastern religions of Hinduism and Buddhism were followed by greater numbers of devotees.

We have called this period the first real millennium because the year 1000 may have had a special importance to the Christians, since it marked the one thousandth anniversary of the traditional year of the birth of Jesus. In biblical times, one thousand was also the highest number with a specific name, since there was little occasion then to count anything that was more than a few thousand. Consequently, when the biblical writers wanted to use a large number, the term "thousand" would be employed.

The book of Revelation, the last book of the New Testament, contains a confusing statement (Chapter 20, Verses 1–3) to the effect that Satan will be bound for a thousand years (that is, an indefinitely long time) and will then be loosed. After that, there will be a final battle in which good overcomes evil at last. The world will then come to an end, giving way to a new heaven and new earth that is perfect and eternal.

Some of those who accepted the word of the Bible literally thought that the end of all things would therefore come to pass in the year 1000. In addition, it must have seemed portentous just to be approaching the first thousand years since the birth of Christ, and to be conscious of that fact.

In later years, the belief developed that the people of that time became extremely agitated about the approach of a new millennium. They supposedly gave everything they owned to the poor, took pilgrimages to Jerusalem, and allowed churches and homes to decay because there was no reason to repair things when the end was so close. Later historians, such as Hillel Schwarz, have suggested that while there was concern at the time, it was not nearly so widespread as legend tells us.

In any event, as we can attest, the world did not come to an end as 999 passed into 1000. Metaphorically, we can now see that the old ways were passing away, as the Dark Ages truly began to lift, and the Renaissance loomed on the horizon, but Earth remained in its orbit and humanity continued its evolution much as it had in the past.

The confused remarks of Revelation continued to cause some

believers to calculate and recalculate when the end of the world would come. Such *millennarians* (from the Latin word for "thousand years") are still with us, but their predictions of a coming end of the world have yet to prove accurate. Undoubtedly, some of the emotions that pervade human beings as the year 2000 approaches may be the result of an uneasy concern that this is the year that really will mark an end.

Islam Asserts Itself

EARLY IN THE MILLENNIUM, IT SEEMED AS IF EVENTS IN WESTern Asia would follow the old pattern of empires rising and falling, rising and falling. We have already noted that the Parthian Empire became the Persian Empire again in 236, and it was successful. Under Khosrow I, the nation's finances were reorganized, Zoroastrianism reformed, and a golden age of art and literature inaugurated. Before being defeated by Heraclius, this Neo-Persian Empire almost overcame the East Roman Empire.

However, a more powerful force was emerging in the region, a new religion whose influence remains extraordinary even today. Just as Judea brought forth something new in the Christian religion, so did Arabia give birth to Islam. Islam (meaning "submission"; that is, to the will of God) was founded by the prophet Muhammad (570–632), who preached the new religion based on revelations and his understanding of Judaism and Christianity.

Birth of Muhammad, founder of Islam

Its practitioners were known as Muslims, ("those who submitted"), and by the time of Muhammad's death in 632, all of Arabia had become Islamic. Islam then spread northward and westward beyond the borders of Arabia. In an extraordinary career of conquest, the Muslims had defeated the Persian Empire and East Roman Empire by 642. Carthage was taken in 698, and by 705 the Muslims had advanced the full width of North Africa and reached the Atlantic Ocean. In 711, they crossed the Strait of Gibraltar and took Spain.

As we have already recounted, the Muslim drive was halted in the east in 718 when they failed to take Constantinople, and in the west at the Battle of Tours in 732.

Nevertheless, by a mere century after Muhammad's death,

Islam controlled an area stretching from the Indus River to the Atlantic Ocean. It was larger than the Roman Empire had been, but less populous because it included so many sparsely settled desert areas.

Almost from the beginning, Islam broke up into sects, as Christianity had done. These groups fought one another, and wars raged between competing families. Much of the Islamic movement's strength was dissipated in this fashion.

The first rulers of Islam were members of the Omayyad family, who had their capital at Damascus. In 750, a competing family, the Abbasids, took over and established Baghdad on the banks of the Tigris as a new capital.

Under the Abassids the Muslims continued to expand, taking several possessions from the Byzantine Empire. They even raided the Italian coastline and sacked Rome itself in 846. The Abbasid Empire was ruled by Harun ar-Rashid (736–809) who came to power in 786. He is the famous ruler who plays a part in the tales of *The Arabian Nights*.

Under the reign of Harun's son, Al-Mamun (746–833), the Abassid Empire peaked. After his departure, however, it fragmented and collapsed.

By the year 1000, although all the earlier conquests remained Muslim, the empire, still under the theoretical control of the ruler in Baghdad, was divided into many small segments. Each was ruled by a separate family, who were quite as likely to fight one another as to fight the Christians. Islam remained a formidable force, but its danger to Europe and to Christianity had become far less acute.

The Orient: Cycles of Feudalism and Unity

FOR THE MOST PART, INDIA REMAINED DIVIDED IN THE FIRST millennium A.D., although occasional strong rulers managed to unite much of it. For example, Chandragupta I, who came to power in 320 when the Roman Empire was becoming Christian, united much of northern India. It remained intact under his immediate successors. Later, Harsha, who ruled from 606 to 647 when the East Roman Empire was fighting off Persia and Islam, established a strong north-Indian state and established contacts with China.

None of these unions persisted for long, however, and after the Muslims conquered Persia, they began raiding northwestern India. In what is now Afghanistan, the Muslim ruler Mahmud of Ghanzi came to power in 997, invading northern India a total of seventeen times.

By the year 1000, India was about to receive a strong infusion of Islam, which would lead eventually to its division into Hindu and Muslim populations, and its ultimate fragmentation into two nations.

China was united under the Han dynasty during the heyday of the Roman Empire, but that came to an end in 220 as the Romans were beginning to feel the impact of tribal invasions.

There then followed four centuries of feudalism and competing dynasties governing separate kingdoms that quarreled among themselves. During this period, Buddhism, transported from India, also flourished in China. The feudal times were reversed when China was reunited in 618 under the T'ang dynasty.

Emperor T'ai Tsung (627–649) of the T'ang dynasty ruled when Islam was beginning its rapid expansion, and he brought many positive changes to China. He welcomed the first Christians to his realm (though they were Nestorians, considered to be heretics by both Rome and Constantinople), and he was also the Chinese ruler who opened up contacts with India. Under this emperor and his successors, China grew rich in art and literature and became technologically advanced.

The T'ang dynasty ended in 907 and was followed by a brief period of renewed feudalism. Northern China came under the rule of a tribe known as the Khitan Mongols, who themselves adopted Chinese culture rapidly. Most of China then came under the native Sung dynasty, which continued to encourage the cultural and technological advances made under their predecessors.

By A.D. 1000, China, under the Khitans and Sungs, had reached a population level of over 60 million and was easily the most technologically and culturally advanced region of the world.

China most advanced region of the world, with population of 60 million

Not far away, Japan, the generally isolated island culture, was adopting Chinese ways and was coming under the control of the Fujiwara family.

Growth Continues Elsewhere

WHILE OUR ATTENTION HAS BEEN FOCUSED ON THE AREAS where the dominant civilizations ebbed and flowed, there continued to be significant developments in other parts of the world. In Africa, the kingdom of Ghana on the western bulge of the continent reached a high level of development in the year 1000. It stretched from the Atlantic Ocean nearly to Timbuktu, trading with northern Africa across the Sahara Desert.

In Central America in 1000, there were several active civilizations exerting strong influence over the region. Around this time, the Mayans, astronomers and builders of cities and ziggurats, had mysteriously begun to abandon those centers and fade into the jungles. In the South Pacific, the intrepid explorers of Polynesia had reached virtually all the islands of that ocean, including Hawaii and Easter Island.

As this first millennium after Christ drew to a close, then, civilization stretched in a broad band across the mid-Northern Hemisphere from the Pacific Ocean to the Atlantic. Going from east to west, the band included Japan, China, India, the Muslim world, the Byzantine Empire, and western Europe. There were also isolated pockets of civilization in tropical Africa and Central America.

World population at 265 million

Humanity was now a major presence on planet Earth. The population was about 265 million, of which some 65 million were in China and nearly 80 million in India. Together, they made up over half the Earth's population and each had an advanced culture and civilization of their own. China's culture was probably the highest in the world at the time.

Farther west, the Byzantine Empire still preserved the complete heritage of Graeco-Roman civilization, while the Muslim world had translated many of the Greek classics into Arabic and maintained a high scholarly culture of their own.

Only western Europe had endured a five-century dark age. It

had lost most of its Greek heritage and in 1000 was by far the least important of the areas of civilization. No one, looking at the world as a whole in 1000, could have guessed that it would be western Europe that would dominate the planet in the course of the next thousand years.

CHAPTER SIX

TECHNOLOGY PROPELS HISTORY
APPROACHING A.D. 2000

THE GREAT TRANSFORMATIONS THAT HAVE TAKEN PLACE ON Earth from A.D. 1000 to the final years of the second millennium A.D. would have been difficult to foresee some 900 years ago. In particular, political struggles and religious differences were at the forefront of the world's thoughts at that time. The impact of technology was frequently felt and created significant changes, but it did not dominate the world civilization as it does today. Science, which is the necessary precursor to such technological development, also did not exist as humanity said goodbye to the first millennium A.D. and looked ahead to the second.

In the millennium approaching A.D. 2000, the greatest technological innovations of humanity have taken place—automobiles, airplanes, computers, nuclear weapons, electricity, radio, television, space travel, genetic engineering. In fact, all of these inventions have taken place in the past hundred years of this millennium. As in the past, such innovations provide the foundation for supporting greater populations, and the planet now houses a human population that would have been unimaginable not long ago.

There were hints of these possibilities one thousand years ago, but only a few.

Western Europe Rallies

THE TURNING POINT IN WESTERN EUROPEAN DEVELOPMENT came with an offensive eastward against the Muslims controlling Palestine (the Holy Land). As the millennium began, the Seljuk Turks had taken over Palestine. They were less civilized and more fanatical than their predecessors, and Christian pilgrims began returning from the Holy Land with atrocity stories.

The Byzantine Empire, under attack by the Turks, was calling for help as well. Meanwhile, the populations of Germany and France were growing and larger numbers of aristocracy were fighting over areas of land that remained finite in size. It was a good time for some of them to be siphoned off to the east, and many nobles saw their opportunity.

Crusades begin; Europeans come into contact with other cultures and rediscover ancient knowledge

Initiated originally by an itinerant preacher known as Peter the Hermit, the Crusades (from a word for "cross" to indicate the Christian purpose of the wars) began in 1096, with the goal of liberating the Holy Land.

Because the Muslim world was divided, the westerners won unexpected victories and succeeded in capturing Jerusalem in 1099. There were several other crusades after the first one, but the Muslims rallied, and in the course of the next two centuries evicted the crusaders from Palestine. The last European stronghold at Acre fell to the Muslims in 1291.

Militarily, the Crusades proved to be a failure, then. In fact, the most significant military result was the weakening and virtual destruction of the (Christian) Byzantine Empire, while the Muslims remained as strong as ever.

In terms of social development, however, the Crusades were a huge success, since western Europeans were for the first time in centuries brought face to face with civilizations superior to their own—the Byzantines and Muslims. The crusaders lost some of their self-satisfaction and learned not only new military tech-niques but also gained an appreciation for luxuries such as sugar and silk. They even came to respect the value of scholarship once again.

During the period of the Crusades, western European scholars gained a new understanding of the neglected knowledge of the past and started translating into Latin the Arabic versions of the Greek scientific and philosophic classics. Spain was the best place to do this work, where the Muslim Moors were still in control of the southern half of the country. There, the level of culture and prosperity was higher than anywhere else in the west, the Arabic translations of the Greek classics could be found, and there were Muslim scholars to help with the work.

Slowly, then, western Europe regained the ancient learning, even though that had not been their original purpose. Militarily, western Europe remained divided and weak and for centuries could only barely fight off invaders from the east. Europe's worst experience of this sort occurred after 1206, when the tribes of central Asia united under Genghis Khan, a military genius of the first order.

He welded together an amazing army of horsemen and began a career of conquest that continued under his sons and grandsons. In 1240 and 1241 the Mongol armies smashed through eastern Europe, penetrating into Germany and reaching the Italian bor-der. They might have gone straight to the Atlantic, but their ruler, a son of Genghis Khan, died, and the armies had to return to elect his successor. **Mongols invade Europe**

Even that disaster had its useful elements for the Europeans. The Mongols established a huge empire stretching from the Danube River to the Pacific Ocean during the latter half of the 1200s. It was ruled by Kublai Khan, a grandson of Genghis Khan. Across this vast empire, united for the first and only time in history, there was free movement of trade and ideas. It was at this time that all sorts of technological innovations traveled from the advanced culture of China to the backward culture of Europe. **Kublai Khan rules China**

The most important of these were the magnetic compass and gunpowder. They allowed the Europeans to begin exploring the **Europeans gain knowledge of gunpowder and magnetic compass from China** planet in earnest, and also to dominate those that they encountered in their travels or in war.

It is interesting to note that the Chinese had never exploited their own inventions to the fullest, but the Europeans quickly began using the compass for navigation at sea, and built cannons that could fire projectiles propelled by the gunpowder.

Western Europe also grew increasingly nationalistic during this period. The papacy had struggled with the Holy Roman emperors between 1050 and 1120 over which institution was to be supreme. By and large, the papacy won out. The popes were also greatly strengthened by the leadership they showed during the Crusades. Under Pope Innocent III, who held the papal chair from 1198 to 1216, the papacy stood at the peak of its power.

Papal claims reached ever greater heights until 1302 when Pope Boniface VIII claimed outright papal superiority over all the kings of Christendom. By that time, France was under a strong king, Philip IV. He sent troops to humiliate Boniface, and forced his successor to move the papal seat from Rome to Avignon in French territory. The papacy never entirely recovered from this defeat, and while it remained influential down to modern times, the power had clearly shifted from church to state.

England conquered by William I of Normandy

Nationalism kept western Europe in a constant state of military turmoil. In 1066, for example, Saxon England was conquered by William I of Normandy (William the Conqueror) who ruled first Normandy and then England from 1035 to 1087. The Normans established a strong monarchy in England and fought constantly with France thereafter.

Hundred Years' War begins

In 1338, the Hundred Years' War began between England and France. The English, making extensive use of the longbow, won significant victories, including the Battle of Agincourt in 1415.

However, the English advantage was blunted by a most unusual development. A young woman, who came to be known as Joan of Arc, claimed to hear and see visions that inspired her to lead the resistance among the French. While the king and nobles resented her efforts, and the church found her to be dangerous, the morale of the people was in fact improved by her efforts. The French also benefited from a more practical development—using improved artillery, as well as Joan's inspiration, they managed to drive the English out of France by 1453.

While the English and French were wasting their resources in war, Italy was going in a different direction. The impact of the rediscovery of Greek learning had great impact here, and culture reached heights in Italy unknown since the days of Periclean Athens. A new emphasis on the human as opposed to the supernatural (humanism) produced the Renaissance (rebirth), and some of the greatest art and literature of all time began to be produced in the city-states of the Italian peninsula.

Renaissance begins in Italy (approximate date)

The city of Florence led the way to become a new Athens. It was at this time that Italians began to equate their own age with that of the ancients, and to characterize the preceding period as the Middle Ages.

Renaissance Italy, like ancient Greece, was by no means the perfect society. It was divided into a number of small states perpetually at war with one another. Like Greece, they eventually fell prey to to the larger powers on their outskirts. The invasions of the French, Germans, and Spanish, beginning in 1494, slowly put an end to the Italian Renaissance, but the new thinking had already spread to the rest of Europe.

All of the discoveries made at this time were not artistic or intellectual, however. Prince Henry (the Navigator) of Portugal conceived the notion of bypassing the Muslim world and trading directly with the Far East by sailing around the tip of Africa. In this way, the Asian products coveted by Europeans could be obtained without obstacles and by avoiding payments to middlemen.

Henry set up a school to study navigation and other new developments in the technology of seafaring. Making use of the magnetic compass and other methods, Prince Henry sent out expedition after expedition to explore the African coast. It was not until 1497, long after Henry's death, that his goal was realized, and Portuguese ships sailed around Africa, reaching India by the new route.

Now, something new came into being, pioneered by the Portuguese and made possible by the new technologies—a world empire based on ships and ocean travel. The ships gave Portugal mobility so that it could establish trading bases all along the shores of Africa and Asia. With cannon, these ships could enforce Portuguese power against peoples who did not have gunpowder.

Meanwhile, the Christian monarchs of Spain had finally completed the expulsion of the Moors in 1492, and in the euphoria of victory, agreed to back the plan of Christopher Columbus to reach Asia by sailing directly west across the Atlantic.

Columbus reaches the "New World"

Columbus had been inspired by Greek geographers who thought the earth was smaller than it really was, and by Marco Polo's book about his visits to the China of Kublai Khan. Polo thought that Asia extended farther east than it really did. Columbus believed that a voyage of 3,000 miles would bring him to Asia. As it turned out, the trip did bring him to land, but that land was not Asia. It was, instead, part of a New World—the North and South American continents.

Aztecs conquered

Spain used Columbus's voyages to begin building its own world empire, based largely on the Americas, where its conquistadores captured and destroyed the Aztec civilization in Mexico in 1519,

Incas conquered

and the Inca civilization in the South American Andes in 1533.

Now began a "great age of exploration," with European powers financing voyages to many parts of the planet. However, the empires could not endure. Portugal was too small, with a population in 1500 of only 1.25 million, to maintain a large empire against the competition of other powers. Spain was larger, with a population of 6.5 million, but it was also engaged in constant warfare in Europe, and that overstrained its capacities.

The Portuguese and Spanish Empires grew increasingly moribund after 1600, and other nations became stronger and more prominent in the exploratory enterprise.

The Netherlands did engage in exploration, but it was also too small to maintain an empire for long. Thus, it was left to France and England to fight it out for world mastery.

France was the larger power, with a population of nearly 20 million in 1600, as compared with 6 million for England. But, like Spain, France was always at war in Europe. England, or Great Britain, as it was called after 1707, was an island less given to continental wars. It was natural for the English to concentrate on overseas trade and empire building.

The decisive period came in the Seven Years' War, fought from 1759 to 1763. At the end of that conflict, Great Britain had evicted France from North America and India. From that time on, the British Empire was the most powerful in the world, reaching its peak in the first half of the 1900s, when it included one-quarter of the world's land and population.

As in other eras, when great changes occurred in one dimension of human life, they seemed to reverberate in others simultaneously. During the time when overseas expansion was beginning, Europe was also shaken by a religious revolution. Led by a monk named Martin Luther, a movement arose in Germany aimed at reforming the Roman Catholic Church. When this was resisted, large numbers of people broke away from Catholicism altogether and formed various denominations of what are now Protestants. Scandinavia, northern Germany, the Netherlands, Bohemia, and Great Britian were lost to the papacy more or less permanently.

Technology once again played a critical role in these social changes. Protestants believed that it was not necessary to have the intercession of priests and other mechanisms of the Catholic Church to be saved. They depended primarily on the word of God, as revealed in the Bible, for their guidance. Gutenberg's invention of the printing press in 1450 made it a realistic goal for all people to have access to "the word," and it is no accident that the Bible was the first book that Gutenberg produced.

Gutenberg invents printing press

The competing religious groups hated each other intensely, and religious differences now became a new rationale for war. The Wars of Religion reached their climax with the Thirty Years' War in Germany, which raged from 1618 to 1648. After that, the contending groups realized the futility of their constant fighting. Except for certain places such as Northern Ireland, they have lived together since then in a kind of grudging peace.

Along with the weakening of the power of the church, there came a slow erosion of the monarchy during this dynamic time. Monarchical nationalism had reached its peak during the autocratic rule of Louis XIV of France from 1643 to 1715, the longest

Reign of Louis XIV begins in France

reign in European history. However, as knowledge and new ideas began to swirl through Europe, the monarchies had to contend with the same problems as the church and other hierarchical organizations. People had begun to think for themselves, and they wanted political systems that allowed them to.

In 1642, England and Scotland rose against the arbitrary rule of Charles I. He was beheaded in 1649, and England had no king for eleven years. After those years of civil strife, Charles I's son was restored (the Restoration) in 1660 and ruled as Charles II. However, his brother and successor James II was removed from the throne in 1688, and England came under the rule of a limited monarchy.

"Glorious Revolution" brings limited monarchical rule to England

This was known as the Glorious Revolution, and it did lay the groundwork for an important new form of government—the limited monarchy coupled with parliamentary government. England had found a formula for legitimacy that synthesized the old (royalty deriving authority from a connection with the Divine) and the new (representatives who derive their authority from the will of the people).

French Revolution

The autocratic monarchy of France could not withstand the changes taking place in England and America, where an even more radical commitment to representative government was being made. In 1789, the year in which the Constitution of the United States was ratified, the French Revolution overthrew the monarchy.

The original French Revolution was dedicated to the "rights of man" and to "liberty, fraternity, and equality." It was indeed an event that might be important enough to inaugurate a new calendar based on it. However, the revolution reeled out of control and became "the terror." The mobs put many aristocrats, including the king and queen, to death.

The French Revolution was also an expansionist movement. Its leaders, in a foreshadowing of later revolutionaries, intended to export its ideals by force of arms. In a precursor to the military draft, it was considered that citizens had an obligation to serve in the army, rather than have the nation depend on mercenaries and professionals. This provided the French with an enormous reservoir of manpower, and made them a formidable enemy.

A series of wars followed, as the kings ruling the rest of Europe desperately tried to contain and reverse the French Revolution. In 1796, their hopes were dealt a great blow when a military genius, Napoleon Bonaparte (1760–1821), began leading the French forces to spectacular victories. Between 1807 and 1811, he succeeded in bringing all of western Europe under his control; only Great Britain remained free.

Napoleon became the emperor of France, reversing the democratic hopes of the revolution, but a welcome change for those who sought stability and glory rather than freedom and justice. As we have seen time and again, however, it is often just at the moment of their greatest power that leaders make the mistakes that bring them down.

In Napoleon's case, it was his invasion of Russia in 1812 that **Napoleon invades** defeated him. While Russia was a backward country with little **Russia** ability to defend itself against the superior French forces, it did have allies that could not be beaten—the Russian space and the Russian winter. The Russian generals withdrew as the French advanced, destroying everything in their path, an early example of the "scorched earth" strategy.

Although Napoleon actually did reach Moscow, he was forced to retreat as the winter snows fell, and his troops grew cold, hungry, and short of supplies and were virtually destroyed. On his return to France, he fought for two more years and was then forced to abdicate. He seized the throne again in the following year, and once again took to the battlefield to prove his worth. He was defeated by the British General Wellington at the Battle of Waterloo and sent into permanent exile.

Napoleon was defeated and the French Revolution sidetracked, but the ideas behind the revolution had been carried over much of the world by the French Army. The victorious monarchs tried to reestablish absolutism. However, they found that they had won the battle but lost the war. They faced a series of revolts in the remainder of the 1800s, and as the 1900s began, parliamentary governments of various degrees of effectiveness had become the standard throughout western Europe.

The major challenge to democratic governments now shifted, coming from the left rather than the right, as intellectuals such as

Karl Marx began developing new theories of society that called for the overthrow of royalty and bourgeois democracy alike.

The Other Revolutions

POLITICAL REVOLUTIONS, AS WE HAVE SEEN, HAVE BEEN A constant feature of the human social landscape for millennia. Sometimes, they make a major difference, and sometimes they do not.

Two revolutions took place in western Europe during the previous centuries of this millennium that are at least as important as the political upheavals of the time. The first of these was the scientific revolution, and the second was the industrial revolution. They were closely linked to the slowly growing importance of the middle classes, who began to think and act creatively. They were also closely related to one another, because the industrial revolution would probably not have taken place without the scientific enterprise as a foundation.

Copernican Revolution: Copernicus develops model of the solar system with sun at center

The seeds for the scientific revolution had been planted during the Renaissance, but they truly burst forth in 1543, when the Polish astronomer, Nicolaus Copernicus (1473–1543) broke with Greek astronomy and asserted that the earth and other planets revolved around the sun, and demonstrated how this more closely fit the observed facts. The Copernican view of the universe was not a small change in perspective, but a radical new cosmology. Adopting it meant rearranging many other ideas about the nature of the universe and humanity.

The importance of the shift is demonstrated by the fact that the Roman Catholic Church forced Galileo Galilei (1564–1642) to recant his statements supporting the Copernican model, which had removed Earth from the center of God's creation.

Galileo uses telescope to discover moons of Jupiter

However, the church could not stop the scientific revolution, nor could anyone else. Galileo studied gravity by experimenting with bodies rolling down an inclined plane. He was also the first person to use the telescope for astronomical observations, discovering four of the moons of Jupiter, among other things. Sir Isaac

Isaac Newton formulates the theory of universal gravitation

Newton (1642–1727) built on the work of Galileo and others to establish the basic laws of motion, and the theory of universal gravitation.

The scientific revolution was revolutionary because it substituted a new way of thinking—the scientific method—for the church's emphasis on faith and truth revealed through scriptures, and the old philosophers' focus on abstract reasoning. The new scientists argued that one must develop theories about the nature of things by observing nature. These theories then had to be tested empirically to determine their truth; experimentation rather than pure thought became the standard for truth.

The scientific revolution has continued and accelerated ever since the sixteenth century, and as the year 2000 approaches, we have worked out atomic structure, developed relativity and quantum theory, understand the laws of thermodynamics, and have begun theorizing about the beginnings of the universe itself.

A second revolution, equally important, was the industrial revolution. It is usually considered to have begun in 1765 with the invention of the modern condensing steam engine by the Scottish engineer, James Watt (1736–1819).

> Industrial Revolution begins with invention of steam engine by James Watt

Humanity's original ability to control fire (combustion) made civilization possible. The steam engine now made it possible to convert the energy of burning fuel into useful work, laying the groundwork for establishing industrial civilization.

A NEW CLASS OF ENTREPRENEURS ESTABLISHED FACTORIES where powered machinery did the work of human hands, increasing productivity enormously. Other sources of energy were found in electricity and the internal combustion engine. Once the industrial revolution got under way, it accelerated until, approaching the year 2000, we now have television, radio, spaceships, and nuclear power as our tools. In a few millennia, humans have gone from making pottery to making computers, from the Bronze Age to the Space Age. We can only guess where these revolutions will lead us, but it is clear that technology is propelling history forward as no other force ever has.

> Britain Takes the Lead

The industrial revolution, beginning as it did in Great Britain, greatly increased British wealth and power and its ability to control the seas, monopolize trade, and further build its empire. It was not the first empire built by a nation that had gained a technological advantage over its competitiors, but it was certainly one of the most successful.

The industrial revolution spread to the rest of Europe, so that through the 1800s, Europe became supreme in the world and European history seemed to become world history.

By the mid-1800s, India was entirely under British control. In the last half of that century, the vast continent of Africa was partitioned almost completely and placed under the control of various European powers.

European colonialism accelerated in the nineteenth century, and affected many other civilizations. China found itself under constant pressure from the European powers, forced to make concession after concession to them. Having exported rather than exploited their own inventions of the compass and gunpowder, the Chinese now found their ideas working against them.

Japan opened up to the West   Then, in 1854, American ships forced the previously closed society of Japan to open itself to international trade. Japan had resisted the new ideas and new technologies of the West for some time, but finally it was forced to adapt. Eventually, Japan found adopting western ways could be to their advantage, and they joined in the plundering of China.

During the 1800s, the city-states of Italy and Germany united to form nations, fundamentally shifting the European balance of power. Germany became the strongest military power in Europe, defeating France in 1870 even before it had become a fully unified nation.

Between 1870 and 1914, Europe, even while achieving world supremacy, consisted of great powers (and small powers) that jockeyed endlessly for advantage over one another. They created complex alliances that none of them completely understood, and laid the groundwork for the disaster that eventually ensued.

On a large scale, Europe was repeating the mistake of the ancient Greeks and Renaissance Italians by maintaining themselves as quarreling units that could not easily combine or cooperate for mutual advantage.

The first half of the twentieth century brought on what amounted to a European civil war that engulfed the planet. In two

colossal struggles, World War I (1914–1918) and World War II
(1939–1945), Germany won initial victories, only to go down to
ignominious defeat. The two wars exhausted the victors as well,
and by 1945 Europe was in ruins.

First World War
begins

World War I ends

These wars represented the most comprehensive example of
what can result from the human tendency to settle disputes by
the use of force. The causes of these wars were not so different
from those of the eighth or seventh millennia B.C. However, the
technology of the twentieth century meant that for the first time,
regional conflicts could escalate to include all of humanity.

The invention, and use, of the nuclear bomb by the United
States further ensured that no one would be able to escape the
consequences of a World War III.

After World War II, Europe's recovery was engineered by the
one power that emerged from the struggle relatively unscathed—
the United States. Europe did revive, but the war ended the
dominance of the Europeans over other parts of the world.

The overseas empires could no longer be maintained, and the
various colonies in Africa, Asia, and elsewhere obtained their
independence soon after World War II. The disintegration of
these empires resulted partially from the exhaustion of the imperial powers, and partially because the war, having been fought for
freedom and democracy, simply reinforced the desire for liberation within the colonies.

As in previous millennia, and even with the force of advanced
technology on their side, empires had proved once again to be
unstable political systems, constantly threatening to fragment. In
1989, even the empire built up by the Soviet Union crumbled.

As the year 2000 approaches, then, Europe clearly no longer
dominates the world, having lost in twenty-five years the empires
it took 450 years to acquire. Europe remains, however, a strong
economic unit, still advanced technologically, mature politically
and surprisingly prosperous.

In addition, the dream of European unity is close to realization
as many of the barriers between the European nations will be
removed in 1992 as part of the evolution of the European
community. The revolutionary changes in eastern Europe open

up the possibility for a united Europe from the Atlantic to the Urals.

Eastern Europe Struggles

WHEN THE WEST ROMAN EMPIRE FELL, THE EAST ROMAN Empire remained standing. It was the eastern empire's ability to maintain ancient Greek knowledge that allowed western Europe to climb out of the Dark Ages and begin the age of exploration, as well as the scientific and industrial revolutions. However, the favor was not easily returned, and eastern Europe has struggled to be successful throughout this millennium.

Schism between Roman Catholic and Greek Orthodox churches

The difficulties began for the Byzantine Empire in the early days of this millennium. In 1025, when Basil II died, no strong successors followed him. The strength of the empire was then wasted away in political infighting for many years. In 1054, the church at Constantinople broke away from the Roman church and Christianity divided in two. This great schism between Roman Catholicism and Greek Orthodoxy has yet to be healed.

By 1071, internal quarreling had ruined the empire. The Byzantine emperor Romanus IV met the Seljuk Turks in the Battle of Manzikert in eastern Asia Minor, and was defeated. More important than the defeat was the cause—key contingents of the Byzantine army simply refused to fight.

The Turks, who were Muslim, took over most of Asia Minor, and the Byzantine Empire permanently lost its status as a great power. From then on, it could only hope to stave off the Muslim onslaught by appealing to western Europe for help.

Crusaders sack Constantinople

As we already know, the western response to these pleas was the Crusades. In the end, however, they did more harm than good as far as the Byzantine Empire was concerned. In 1204, the crusaders turned aside from their stated aim of fighting the Muslims and intervened in a Byzantine civil war. The crusaders took Constantinople and sacked it, destroying the last repository of Greek learning and leaving to the world only scraps of the original knowledge, mostly portions that Muslims had been able to translate.

Ironically, the Byzantines' rescuers had done exactly what they had been called upon to prevent—the destruction of the empire. The crusaders then set up a short-lived Latin empire. The Byzantines did not give up, however, and they were able to regain Constantinople in 1261. However, the empire was now only a shoddy imitation of what it once had been. A new tribe of Turks, the Ottomans, were now in the ascendancy in Asia Minor, while the Bulgars and Serbs took over the Balkan peninsula.

In 1354, the Ottoman Turks crossed over into Europe and began to spread throughout the Balkans. That invasion ushered in the final century of the Byzantine Empire. In 1453, the Turks took Constantinople at last and the grand Roman tradition, which could trace itself back to the founding of Rome twenty-two centuries earlier, had ended. Rome had finally fallen.

Fall of Constantinople to the Turks

Still, Russia remained to carry on a version of the Byzantine tradition. Russia was Greek Orthodox in religion, and in 1000 it formed a strong monarchy in what is now the Ukraine, with its capital at Kiev.

In 1237, however, the Mongol armies swept in from the east and conquered Kievan Russia and virtually all the rest of the country. For 150 years, Russia suffered under the Mongol (or Tartar) yoke, separated from the rest of Europe and missing out on the important cultural developments in the west, especially the Renaissance.

In 1380, the prince of Moscow, Dmitri, inflicted the first defeat on the Tartars at the Battle of Kulikovo. The struggle continued under the lead of Moscow, and under Ivan III, who ruled from 1462 to 1505, the Tartars were finally defeated. Russia ruled its own destiny once again.

In 1472, Ivan III had married Zoe (Sophia), who was the niece of Constantine XI, the last of the Byzantine emperors. Ivan felt that this made him the heir of the Roman tradition. He adopted the title of czar or tsar (a Russian version of Ceasar), and Moscow was considered the "third Rome," after Rome itself and Constantinople.

Under Ivan IV (the Terrible), who reigned from 1533 to 1548, Russia began to come together as a nation. The Russian principal-

Reign of "Ivan the Terrible" begins in Russia

ities were all united, including the thinly populated northern territories bordering on the Artic Ocean. In the 1550s, what remained of Tartar territory in eastern Russia was conquered, and Moscow ruled the entire course of the Volga River to the Caspian Sea. Geographically, Russia was the largest country in Europe at this time; however, it was very thinly populated, with some 10 million people in 1600, about half the population of France.

After Ivan IV's death, Russia went through a "time of troubles," but it held together until 1613, when a new dynasty, the Romanovs, came to the throne. A pattern now emerged, which has continued ever since, of strong Russian leaders vigorously attempting to bring backward Russia up to the level of the West, often by adopting western ways, sometimes by competing against the West.

Peter the Great attempts to Westernize Russia

In 1689, Peter I (the Great) became tsar and was an exemplification of this model. He was a man of superabundant energy who worked hard to westernize Russia. He introduced western customs, science, and culture, and founded a new capital at St. Petersburg on the western borders of Russia. He also defeated the Swedes in 1709 at the Battle of Poltava in the Ukraine. This was important because the Swedes had been the great power of the north for some seventy years, but Russia now replaced Sweden in that role.

As early as the 1580s, Russian fur traders had made their way east of the Urals into Siberia, and they continued to press eastward in the time of Peter the Great. They reached the Pacific Ocean, and Russia then became the largest contiguous realm in the world. It has retained that standing ever since.

Russia expanded into Europe as well. During the reign of Catherine II, from 1762 to 1796, Russia took the northern shores of the Black Sea from the Turks and the eastern half of Poland when that nation was partitioned with Prussia and Austria.

Russia reached the peak of its European influence in 1812, when Napoleon invaded and met disaster. The next year, Russia joined with Austria and Prussia to move westward; by 1814, Russian forces were in Paris and Napoleon was out.

The Russian victory was a defeat in other ways, because it was thereafter the mainstay of despotism in Europe. While revolutions shook western Europe, Russia remained firmly autocratic. The industrial revolution moved western Europe forward, but Russia remained largely unaffected. As a result, the nations of western Europe grew steadily stronger while Russia lagged behind, held back not only by its lack of industry, but also by the lack of education and general inefficiency of its government.

Russia was consequently defeated in the Crimean War by Great Britain and France in 1856. Russia did manage to overcome the Turks in 1878, but was not allowed to benefit from the victory because of pressure from the western Europeans. The Russians were even badly beaten by the Japanese in the 1904–05 war.

By that time, the industrial revolution was beginning to take hold, and the educated portion of the nation was pushing hard for reform to take advantage of it. The Japanese defeat set off a revolt that the government barely managed to contain. When, in the course of World War I, Russia was being catastrophically defeated by the Germans, the unrest boiled over again.

Finally, Tsar Nicholas II, who reigned from 1894 to 1917, was forced to abdicate. The Russian Revolution overthrew the rulers, and the most radical of the revolutionaries, the Bolsheviks (a faction of the Communist party), took over after a brief period of democracy. **Russian Revolution**

The western powers tried to throttle the Russian Revolution in its crib, sending invading armies into Russia to stop the Bolsheviks from securing their power. However, the new government survived, establishing a one-party communist state. The Russia of the Tsars remained intact, except for the western border areas, which became the independent states of Poland, Finland, Lithuania, Latvia, and Estonia.

For the next twenty years, the new Union of the Soviet Socialist Republics, or Soviet Union, was an outcast nation.

However, after Germany's defeat in World War I, that nation grew strong again under the nightmarishly repressive regime of Adolf Hitler, who came to power in 1933, and Europe had to realign itself. **Adolf Hitler takes power in Germany**

Great Britain and France desperately needed allies if they were to contain Hitler, and they made halfhearted attempts to draw the Soviet Union into an alliance. The Soviet Union, however, was now under the rigid control of Josef Stalin (1879–1953), who was suspicious of British-French intentions. It shocked the world when the announcement came that he had signed a nonagression pact with his arch-enemies, the Nazis.

The treaty between Hitler and Stalin was a cynical move by both dictators, but it did serve their mutual purposes. The Germans gained two years to focus on attacking the rest of Europe and England without worrying about being attacked from the rear. The Russians gained time to prepare for the eventual invasion by the Germans.

By 1941, Germany had conquered all of western Europe except for Great Britain, as had been true of Napoleon nearly a century and a half earlier. Having failed to overcome Britain, Hitler, like Napoleon before him, made the fateful error of invading the Soviet Union. Once again, after a series of initial victories, and with the Germans on the outskirts of Moscow, the Russian winter hit with a vengeance that halted the German advance.

Like the French, the Germans were forced to retreat slowly and agonizingly through the snow, but they left some 20 million Russians dead behind them. The Soviet Union ended the war victorious but exhausted. It had taken over much of eastern Europe during the final days of the war, but was again an outcast. Western Europe, led by the United States, and eastern Europe, led by the Soviet Union, stood face to face in a "cold war" for some forty years.

The advantage lay with the west, which was a much stronger power economically than the east. However, since both sides had nuclear weapons by the early 1950s, a major war between the two superpowers became virtually impossible.

Thus, the competition has taken place in other countries, sometimes as economic competition, sometimes as open warfare. At times, the superpowers have become engaged, as in Vietnam and Afghanistan, but never in the same place and at the same time.

As the latter decades of the century and the millennium

approached, the Soviet Union had begun to bend under the strain. Its economic problems made reform a necessity, and under Mikhail Gorbachev attempts at reform have gained momentum. One of the most remarkable developments of our time has been the embracing of democracy in eastern Europe, as the nations of the region have begun to break away from Soviet control.

Mikhail Gorbachev takes over in Soviet Union; initiates policies of "glasnost" and "peristroika"

As the year 2000 approaches, it seems clear that the very dangerous cold war is finally over. The victory appears to have gone to the West, as nations all over the world have begun to adopt democratic political systems coupled with free enterprise economics. Nevertheless, the United States itself was not a clear winner, for in the course of the cold war, it was greatly weakened economically and socially.

Eastern Europe moves toward democracy

THE MUSLIM WORLD HAS SEEN A REMARKABLE PERIOD OF evolution during this millennium. In spite of many ups and downs, Islam has shown itself to be an extremely influential force on the world scene.

The Muslim World Has an Impact

The Abassid Empire was fragmented by the year 1000, but the tribes at its fringes had been converted to Islam and the Turkish tribes of central Asia took over portions of the empire, just as seven centuries earlier Germanic tribes had taken over portions of the Roman Empire.

The Seljuk Empire reached its peak after it had defeated the Byzantines, but disintegrated rapidly after 1092, giving the crusaders their chance to take Jerusalem. The Muslim world also suffered from the impact of the apparently irresistible Mongol advance in the mid-1200s.

However, after the crusaders had been defeated and the Mongol Empire had fallen apart, the Ottoman Turks made thier appearance and were very successful. By 1397, they were laying siege to Constantinople and would have taken it but for the appearance of another great conqueror on the scene. Timur the Lame (Tamerlane), who was supposedly a descendant of Genghis Khan, overwhelmed central Asia, smashed the Tartars in Russia, and defeated the Turks in 1402 at the Battle of Angora.

The Ottoman Turks were saved when Tamerlane died as he was marching on China. Their conquest of Constantinople in 1453 made the Ottomans the strongest power in Europe and Islam became a greater threat to Christianity than it had been since the first outward surges of the Arabs. Under Selim I, who reigned from 1512 to 1520, the Turks took Egypt, and their control also spread northward along the shores of the Black Sea.

Under Suleiman I (the Magnificent), who ruled from 1520 to 1566, the Ottoman Empire reached its peak, and he almost succeeded in taking Vienna. After his death, the empire slowly declined, even though they did manage another attack on Vienna. By now, the Turks had fallen well behind western Europe in military strength, and the Austrians launched a counterattack that drove the Turks steadily back.

In 1699, the Turks were forced to sign a treaty ceding Hungary to the Austrians. The Turks then fought a series of losing wars against the Russians; the people of the Balkans, most of whom were Christian, revolted against Turkish rule as well. By 1913, Turkey had been driven from Europe except for the area immediately around Constantinople. By that time, too, their north African dominions had been taken over by the west Europeans. Great Britain claimed Egypt; Italy took Libya; France had Tunisia, Algeria, and Morocco.

In 1914, the Ottoman Turks made the mistake of fighting on the side of the Germans, and they lost again. They gave up Iraq and Palestine to the British, and Syria and Lebanon to the French. Even portions of Asia Minor were assigned to Greece and Italy. However, alone among the losing powers of World War I, Turkey refused to accept defeat.

Under a leader known as Kemal Ataturk (1881–1938), Turkey fought the Greeks and secured a new treaty leaving it in sole control of Asia Minor. Ataturk then forced a series of reforms on Turkey that secularized the country, wiped out the power of Muslim religious leaders, and converted Turkey into a member of the European family of nations.

After World War II, other Muslim nations became independent, including Jordan, Syria, Lebanon, Iraq, Egypt, Libya, Tunisia,

Algeria, and Morocco. The Arab world, or Middle East, gained new importance in the 1940s, when it became apparent that their territories included the largest oil reserves on Earth.

This discovery made the Arabs unexpectedly powerful, because oil is absolutely necessary as an energy source in an industrialized world. They would have been even more powerful if they had been able to unite. However, even the establishment of Israel in 1948 (restoring a Jewish homeland after nearly seventeen centuries), which gave the Arabs a common enemy, did not cause them to come together fully.

In 1979, a form of Muslim fundamentalism seized control of Iran, site of the old Persian Empire. This fundamentalism threatened all of Iran's neighbors, and triggered an inconclusive eight-year war with Iraq. An even longer civil war, involving Christians, Muslims, Palestinians, and Syrians, has torn apart Lebanon. In general, there is unrest throughout the Middle East, including Israel, where Arab territory occupied by the Israelis during the 1967 war is now in a constant state of insurrection, or *Intifadah*.

As we move toward the year 2000, it is difficult to see where the struggles in the Middle East, cradle of civilizations, will end, or how any form of peace can be achieved. However, if there is to be peace in the world, it must include this region or it will never be stable.

India Emerges

AFTER 1000, INDIA CONTINUED TO BE DIVIDED INTO NUMEROUS states, fighting with one another endlessly. The situation was enlivened now and then by a capable ruler who established order over a limited area, an effort that usually ended after his death. India also suffered horrible disasters, as when Tamerlane invaded the north and virtually annihilated Delhi for no apparent reason other than the enjoyment of destruction.

In 1498, the Portuguese explorer, Vasco da Gama (1460–1524) reached India, and the Portuguese immediately began establishing trading stations along the coast. They acquired Goa in 1510 and used it as their chief headquarters. This began a process of European interference in India that lasted for centuries.

Portuguese ships reach India by sailing around Africa

In 1526, Babar (1483–1530), who traced his ancestry back to Genghis Khan, founded the Mogul Empire (a distortion of "Mongol") in India. For a time, India was a powerful country under his rule. The Mogul Empire grew even stronger under Babar's grandson Akbar (1542–1605), who came to the throne in 1556. Despite all the Mogul ability to defeat competing Indian rulers and unite large sections of the land, they could not expel the Portuguese.

Shah Jahan, the grandson of Akbar, is remembered chiefly for having overseen the construction of the Taj Mahal in Agra between 1632 and 1653. This served as a tomb to his wife, Mumtaz Mahal.

The last successful Mogul ruler was Aurangzib, who reigned from 1658 to 1707. By that time, the Portuguese power had ebbed, but now the British had begun to make incursions. They established a post at Bombay in 1661 and began competing with the French, who were also establishing bases in India.

In the 1700s, Great Britain and France were fighting each other in Europe and North America, and this rivalry reflected itself in India, as well. The French administrator Joseph-Francois Dupleix (1697–1763) tried to manipulate internal Indian politics to favor France, but he was outmaneuvered by the British administrator, Robert Clive (1725–1774).

The British had established Calcutta as their base, but in 1756 an Indian ruler of the region had taken Calcutta. According to the story, he imprisoned over one hundred people in a small airless room in the Indian summer heat (the "Black Hole of Calcutta") where most died. Clive then re-took Calcutta in 1757 and defeated the Indian ruler at the Battle of Plassey.

Great Britain then gained control of Bengal and slowly made themselves arbiters of the rest of India, leaving the Mogul emperor still on the throne, but only as a puppet.

By the middle of the nineteenth century, with India almost entirely under British control, there were fears that Russian expansion in central Asia might threaten India. This created an intense hostility toward Russia in Great Britain that lasted for half a century. It also gave rise to British expeditions into Afghanistan to keep that country out of Russian hands.

In 1857, British rule was shaken by the revolt of the Sepoys, Indian soldiers employed by the British. There was a massacre of British women and children, leading to a bitter repression of the revolt by the British army. This event led to the final demise of the Mogul Empire, and the government of Great Britain then took over direct rule of India.

The opening of the Suez Canal in 1869 greatly increased trade between Europe and India and led to a growing Indian prosperity. Economic success made British rule more tolerable, and Queen Victoria was named Empress of India in 1877, replacing the now-defunct line of Mogul monarchs.

The Indians never totally accepted British rule, however, and sentiments for Indian self-government rose during this time. Numerous leaders calling for self-rule and independence appeared, the most important of whom was Mohandas Karamchand Gandhi (1869–1948). Gandhi's leadership of a nonviolent struggle for Indian independence created a model that later found adherents all over the world, including the United States.

During World War I, India loyally supported Great Britain, and British preoccupation with the European theatre of operations led to much greater Indian involvement in their own government. After the war, the British tried to restore the status quo. When the Indians resisted, they introduced harsh measures to suppress antigovernment agitation.

The Indians responded by following Gandhi's strategy; on April 10, 1919, they carried out a day of fasting and a general strike. Despite Gandhi's insistence on nonviolence, there were some Indian attacks on the British. A British officer responded three days later by having his troops fire into an unarmed crowd at Amritsar, killing 379 people and wounding 1,200. The massacre generated new support among the Indians for the independence movement and destroyed all hope of reconciliation. It was only a matter of time before the British would have to agree to independence, though they held to their position for another thirty years.

The Second World War weakened the British so much that they could no longer maintain their empire, and independence for India was clearly close at hand. Now a new threat appeared on the horizon—the growing enmity between the Hindus and Muslims within the Indian population.

In 1946, the British finally offered independence to India, but the Hindus and Muslims could not agree on the final terms for setting up a new state. Even Gandhi could not bridge the gap between the two communities. The only possible solution was partition, the establishing of two nations.

In the final plan, India would be for the Hindus, and Pakistan (a name built up of the initials of constituent regions) would be for the Muslims. Pakistan consisted of two regions a thousand miles apart and separated by India itself. West Pakistan was to be northwest of India and East Pakistan to the northeast.

India becomes independent and is partitioned

The two nations came into being on August 15, 1947, and both remained members of the British Commonwealth of Nations, which was replacing the empire as the form of relationship among former British colonies. Of course, many Hindus lived in the areas that were now known as Pakistan and many Muslims were living in the area to be set up as India. As the masses of people attempted to move from one region to the other, there was massive sectarian strife, and many died.

Jawaharlal Nehru (1889–1964), Gandhi's most important follower, became the first prime minister of India. Gandhi himself was assassinated in 1948 by an extremist Hindu who objected to the partition of India.

India forced the still-existing monarchical states to join the new nation and declared itself a republic in 1950. In 1955, India forcibly annexed Goa, which had been a Portuguese trading center for 450 years.

The Indian subcontinent has been witness to ongoing violence since India gained her independence. India has gone to war with both Pakistan and China, and has faced serious internal problems with the Sikh minority in the north. After Nehru's death in 1966, his daughter, Indira Nehru Gandhi (1917–1984) became prime minister. She took strong measures against the Sikhs, sending troops to invade their holiest temple, on the grounds that it served as a sanctuary for Sikh extremists. In 1984, she was assassinated by members of her Sikh bodyguards and was replaced as president by her son.

As for Pakistan, its split into an "east wing" and a "west wing" did not work well. Not only were the two portions of the land extremely far apart, but East Pakistan felt excluded from the power centers in the west. In 1971, East Pakistan, aided by India, won its independence and created the new nation of Bangladesh.

Approaching the year 2000, the future of the Indian subcontinent remains uncertain. India has emerged as an increasingly modern nation on the world scene, with a booming film industry and growing computer software industry. India is also the world's largest democracy. The country still faces enormous problems, however, because of its large population, many of whom still live in rural poverty. Pakistan is emerging from years of military dictatorship and is one of the more powerful Muslim nations in the world.

Bangladesh, meanwhile, is one of the most densely populated and poorest nations on Earth and is still struggling for survival. The island of Ceylon, off the tip of India, became the independent nation of Sri Lanka in 1948. It has been plagued by civil war for much of its recent history, as the Tamil minority in the north tries to obtain its independence.

While this region will clearly play an important role in the future, it is difficult to predict the exact nature of its contribution.

China: Still One-Fifth of the World's Population

DURING THE THOUSAND YEARS OF THIS MILLENNIUM, CHINA endured many difficult transitions. As the millennium draws to a close, it seems likely that the world's most populous nation has still more political convulsions to endure—with important implications for all of us.

As the millennium opened, most of China had fallen to the Mongol invaders. By 1210, Kublai Khan, who had thoroughly adopted Chinese culture, ruled from Shang-tu, north of present Beijing. His empire included not only China but also central Europe. Following a familiar pattern, however, his expeditions against Japan, southeast Asia, and the Indonesian islands all failed, and Mongol rule did not long survive his death.

In 1368, the Mongols were driven from China, and the Ming dynasty was established. During the reign of the Ming emperor,

Yung Lo, China embarked on an age of exploration that resembled what was taking place in Europe. From 1403 to 1424, Chinese fleets scoured the Indian Ocean, visiting Indonesia, Ceylon, and even the Red Sea.

This activity might have laid the foundation for a world empire centered around coastal bases, but in a classic reversal, China turned inward with the death of Yung Lo. Abandoning exploration, China became isolated and lost its technological superiority.

It was left to the European nations to be the empire builders of that period, and unfortunately for the Chinese, the empires often included their land. A century after the docking of the fleets, Europeans had begun to reach China, and in 1557, the Portuguese had established a trading post at Macao (which it has retained into the latter years of the millennium).

China helped Korea fight off the Japanese in the 1590s, but by then the Ming dynasty had grown weak. Tribes in Manchuria, related to the Mongols, took over the throne in 1644 and established Manchu rule, known as the Ch'ing dynasty.

The early Manchu emperors gave Imperial China its last period of significant power within the community of nations. In 1689, the Chinese forced the Russians to sign a treaty abandoning some of the territories they had taken on the Chinese frontier. Through the 1700s, China was able to expand its influence in Tibet, Burma, and elsewhere, while successfully restricting Europeans to the narrow confines of the established trading centers.

However, it was only a matter of time before internal corruption, combined with the growing technological superiority of the West, would bring on a crisis. It came in 1841 when China tried to stop the opium trade, which was dominated by the British. The British won out in the struggle, continued the opium commerce, and set up a trading post in Hong Kong.

This event began a century of continuing Chinese humiliation at the hands of the more advanced nations. However, many of China's problems were also internal. The declining efficiency of Manchu rule brought about rebellion from the countryside and between 1850 and 1864, the T'ai Ping Rebellion occurred. The central government won out, but not before many people were killed and the country badly weakened.

In the latter half of the 1800s, Great Britain, France, Germany, Russia, and Japan all participated in the continuing exploitation of China. From 1894 to 1895, Japan fought and defeated China, then annexed the island of Taiwan.

The Chinese rose against their occupiers in 1900, in the Boxer Rebellion. This event became a pretext for an international force to move in and put down the uprising, but also to increase control over China. By now, it was clear that Imperial China was dying, and in 1911, a popular revolt drove the Manchus out, leading to the establishment of a Chinese republic.

The republic was itself torn by conflict among the many warlords who controlled regions of the country and maintained their own private armies. The struggle became polarized between Chiang Kai-shek (1887–1975) and Mao Tse-tung (1893–1976). Chiang represented the more conservative interests in China, while Mao became a Communist, working toward revolution, as well as ridding the country of outside intervention.

Of course, it was the Communists who eventually won out, but not without a long struggle. Facing defeat in 1934, Mao led his army on the Long March from the coast to the far northwest region of Shensi, where he established a Communist regime that was maintained for the next fifteen years.

While the Chinese fought among themselves, Japan moved to take over as much of China as possible. The Japanese took over Manchuria in 1930, establishing the puppet regime of Manchukuo. In 1937, Japan drove into northern China and took over Shanghai, Canton, Nanking, and Hankow. The Japanese campaign in China was halted by the advent of World War II, and the final moves in the fight to control China began after the war ended.

Mao Tse-tung, superbly practicing the art of guerrilla warfare, managed to defeat Chiang Kai-shek, in spite of massive American military aid to Chiang. In 1949, Chiang and his forces fled to Taiwan, where they set up a new regime, while Mao established the People's Republic of China on the mainland.

Chinese Communists take over mainland China

Foreign domination was ended with the coming to power of the Communist regime, but China's problems were by no means over. The Chinese intervened in the Korean War in 1950, fighting to a bloody and inconclusive stalemate with the United States and its allies. Tension between China and Taiwan remained high during the 1950s, with the United States supporting Taiwan and the Soviet Union backing the People's Republic.

In the 1960s, however, China broke with the Soviet Union and went its own way, creating a new brand of Communism known as Maoism. China oscillated between periods of hard-line Communism and liberalization, still searching for the best way to rule a vast country with many problems confronting it. For most of the 1950s and 1960s, China continued to be quite isolated from the rest of the world. However, in 1971, the People's Republic was admitted to the United Nations, replacing Taiwan as the representative of China. In 1972, the United States normalized diplomatic relations with the Chinese, further diminishing its separation from the mainstream.

After Mao Tse-tung's death, the new leaders embarked on a program of economic liberalization, allowing a modicum of free enterprise and opening the country up to foreign trade. However, their program did not include political freedom, nor the abrogation of the Communist party's leading role in guiding the nation.

A strong, student-led pro-democracy movement, reflecting trends elsewhere in the world, began to confront the rulers as the 1980s drew to a close. The movement was crushed by troops of the People's Army, who carried out a massacre in Beijing's Tienanmen Square before the shocked eyes of the world, who watched television pictures of the event beamed around the globe via satellite.

As the millennium draws to a close, China remains an unknown variable in the world equation. Under Communism, the country did solve many of its problems, such as how to feed its massive population and how to overcome foreign domination. However, resistance to Communist rule is increasing.

Today, some 1 billion of Earth's 5 billion human beings are Chinese, maintaining the 20 percent proportion established millennia before. As democracy takes hold in almost every other nation of the world, and the youth of China embrace it, the ultimate triumph of the ancient Greeks' political invention seems inevitable. However, nothing is ever truly inevitable in human history, and we will simply have to wait and see how the "China variable" plays itself out in the coming millennium.

___

HE STORY OF JAPAN, LIKE THAT OF CHINA, IS ONE OF *Japan Surges* isolation evolving into emergence as an important world *Forward* power. Like the Chinese, the Japanese people have also gone through many transformations to reach their current status. The major difference is that the Japanese, having been forced to adopt democracy and a free enterprise system after World War II, have become an incredibly successful player on the world economic scene.

Having obtained much of its culture from China, Japan retired into isolation, something that its status as an island nation made possible. Kublai Khan's invasion attempts in 1274 and 1281 failed because violent storms damaged his fleets and forced them to retire. The Japanese always remembered and honored the kamikaze, or divine wind, and would manifest it themselves in a war fought nearly seven hundred years later.

The Portuguese and Spanish invasion of traders and missionaries was more difficult to resist. In 1549, a missionary named Francis Xavier arrived, with the goal of Christianizing the nation. He never completely succeeded but did make significant progress toward his goal.

In the latter half of the 1500s, Japan was effectively unified and the constant fighting among feudal warlords was dampened. In 1585, Hideyoshi Toyotoma (1537–1598), peasant-born but rising in his society because of his political and military genius, became the ruler of all Japan. He initiated an anti-Christian movement that eventually wiped out most of the Christian influence in the course of the next forty years. His efforts to initiate a program of Japanese expansionism in Korea failed, but they were harbingers of things to come.

After Hideyoshi's death, Ieyasu (1543–1616) gradually gained *Shogunate* power until he was appointed shogun (generalissimo) by the *established in Japan* emperor in 1603. He was the effective ruler of Japan under the figurehead emperor, and the shogunate remained in his Tokugawa family for two and a half centuries. He completed the eradication of Christianity, got rid of almost all the foreign traders, and effectively isolated Japan from the rest of the world.

It was out of this isolation and holding to traditional values that the samurai chose to have guns banned, because it gave too much power to the peasantry and removed the honor from battle. This was one of the vanishingly few cases in human history where significant technological advances were deliberately abandoned, and it could be done only because the Japanese had isolated themselves and were not threatened from without.

By the mid-1800s, however, Japanese isolation could no longer be maintained. Western ships now dominated the oceans, and they wanted to bring Japan into the family of nations so that profitable trade relations could be established. In 1853, American ships under Matthew Calbraith Perry (1794–1858) sailed into Tokyo Harbor to demand a trade treaty. He returned the next year, and the Japanese bowed to superior force against their own wishes.

Japan then went through a period of uncertainty. Some dreamed of getting rid of the foreigners again and returning to the traditional policy of isolation. Others were willing to enter into the mainstream and adopt western technology.

Mutsohito (1852–1912) became emperor in 1867, and responded to the reformers who wanted the shogunate ended and with it the Japanese feudal system. Under him, Japan set itself on the path of adopting western technology. The end came in 1877, when an army of samurai, supporting the old ways, were soundly defeated by an army of commoners, armed with modern weapons.

Japan developed a modern army and navy, which enabled it to embark on the expansion program that Hideyoshi had dreamed about three centuries before. The logical prey was China, still mired in its old ways.

Japan's victory over China led to its attacks on Korea and Manchuria, which created the next major conflict—with Russia. Once again, Japan astonished the world by launching a surprise attack on the Russians in 1904, and then defeating them in the war that followed. The resulting peace treaty gave the Japanese the southern half of Sakhalin Island, and in 1910 Japan also annexed Korea.

Japan's expansionism then continued unabated for over forty years, and some western powers might have come to wonder if prying them out of their isolation had been such a good idea. The Japanese were nominal members of the Allied powers during World War I but did little to help the cause except annex some German-dominated islands lying north of the equator.

After World War I, Japan grew more hostile to the western powers, partially because of a desire to supplant them as prime exploiters of China. In 1931, the Japanese invaded Manchuria, and when western opposition proved ineffective, they went on to invade China in 1937.

The French defeat by the Germans in 1940 gave Japan a chance to dominate French Indochina and establish its power in southeastern Asia. The United States was clearly the only western enemy Japan needed to fear. They planned a surprise attack against the United States, modeled on their venture against the Russians in 1904.

The Japanese attack on Pearl Harbor in 1941 caught the American fleet unaware and destroyed much of it. The Japanese were not totally successful only because the American aircraft carriers were away from the base at the time, and they escaped unharmed.

In the following months, Japan took over the Philippine Islands, southeast Asia (including Singapore), and the Dutch East Indies. For a time, it appeared that the Japanese were as formidable in the Pacific as the Germans had been in Europe. However, a turning point came when the Americans defeated the Japanese fleet at the Battle of Midway Island in June 1942.

Just as the Germans were on the defensive once they were defeated in Russia, so were the Japanese driven steadily back after Midway. American forces fought their way up the island chain until they reached the Japanese home islands in mid-1945. The Pacific War ended with the advent of the ultimate achievement in military technological superiority—the nuclear bomb.

Once the bomb had been dropped on Hiroshima and Nagasaki,

Atomic bomb used for first time

the Japanese had no choice but to accept unconditional surrender on September 2, 1945. Japanese expansionism via military force was over, and Japan had its territory reduced to the four islands it had occupied in Commodore Perry's time.

Japan was forced to accept a democratic constitution by the occupying American forces, led by General Douglas MacArthur. It was not allowed to develop armed forces, remaining under the umbrella of American military protection instead. Not having to spend any money on the military and making use of an entirely new industrial plant, the Japanese turned themselves entirely to business and trade.

By the 1980s, Japan had become so successful economically that it was wealthier than the United States in total assets and was outpacing the West in many aspects of technology. The Japanese ability to adopt western technological innovations had reached a high level, as they learned to take the ideas of others and mass-market them at the lowest possible costs.

In some ways, the two apparently contradictory themes of isolation and expansion remain embedded in Japanese thought and policies even today. The Japanese are certainly very involved in commercial activities throughout the world, yet remain an insular and homogeneous society at home and abroad.

As the year 2000 approaches, Japan's control over large quantities of the planet's wealth make it one of the most powerful societies in the world, and decisions made by the Japanese will have a significant effect on the planet's future.

It now seems clear that the Japanese have achieved by peaceful means much of what they failed to accomplish with military might.

A New Nation Leads the World

AS THE YEAR 1000 DAWNED, NO ONE IN EUROPE WOULD have predicted that the course of the last few centuries of the millennium would be dominated by a nation far across the Atlantic Ocean. That would have seemed like a fantasy to the people of that time, because no one even knew of a land across the ocean.

Perhaps a few of the Vikings might have made such a bold prediction, because they had colonized the southwestern shore of Greenland and had made landings in what is now Newfoundland. As far as we know, they were the first Europeans to land in what became known as the New World. However, their colonies did not last, and they did not seem to spread the word of what they had found on their voyages.

Nevertheless, a great deal was already happening in North and South America, even before the Europeans knew about it. The Native American cultures reached considerable levels of sophistication in Mexico, where the Aztecs established an empire, and in the northern Andes of South America, where the Incas lived.

However, the voyages of exploration that were such a powerful stimulus for European society proved to be disastrous for the native civilizations, which were decimated by the arrival of Columbus and those who followed.

During that century, most of the European nations attempted to establish a foothold in the New World, including Spain, France, the Netherlands, Great Britain, and even Sweden. England eventually became the dominant power, forming a solid line of colonies from Maine to South Carolina, plus Newfoundland in what became Canada. The French had expanded westward and by the 1680s had followed the Mississippi River to its mouth. They claimed the entire central portion of what is now the United States in addition to all of eastern Canada.

The English colonies were hemmed in on the Atlantic coast, but they were growing rapidly in population, while the French colonies were sparsely populated. Beginning in 1689, a series of wars between Great Britain and France took place, and some of the battles were fought in North America. The British drove France from the continent, and everything east of the Mississippi and north of the Gulf of Mexico became British. West and south of the British holdings was Latin America, which remained under the control of Spain and Portugal.

Plymouth Colony established in New World

However, Great Britain had accumulated a large national debt as a result of the war and undertook to tax the colonies to raise some of the money for payment. The resistance of the colonies

American
Declaration of
Independence

American colonies
defeat British

U.S. Constitution in
force; George
Washington elected
first president

led to the War of American Independence, with the official
Declaration of Independence in 1776. The American colonies,
with the support of France, managed to defeat the British in
1783, and Great Britain signed a treaty recognizing the independence of the United States in that year.

The United States functioned under an agreement called the
Articles of Confederation until a constitutional convention in
1787 resulted in a written constitution that established a strong
federal government. George Washington, the general who had
led the struggle for American freedom, was elected the first
president of the new country and began his term in 1789.

In the long history of human experimentation with political
systems, the American effort stands out as a major development
that has become a model for many other countries. The separation of the government into three branches guarantees that no
one person or institution can gain too much power. Periodic
elections also help to guard against unwarranted concentrations
of power. The relatively strong central government captures many
of the benefits of centralization disussed earlier, but the Bill of
Rights and the federal nature of the government ensure that
tyranny is difficult, if not impossible, to achieve.

The American system enshrines the democratic ideal of legitimacy flowing from the will of the people, and this is made clear
in the opening words of the Constitution, "We the people . . ."
Moreover, the Constitution clearly separates church and state,
finally abandoning the old approach to legitimacy, that of the
god-king whose authority is derived from a connection to divine
forces.

The American approach is like the Greeks' in its focus on
freedom and democracy, and like the Romans' in its respect for
the rule of law. It seems to borrow from many other systems, and
while it is certainly not a perfect system of government, it has
built into the Constitution clearcut mechanisms for adaptation
and evolution.

Achieving political independence was important, but it was not
enough. The United States benefited enormously when a British
engineer named Samuel Slater smuggled knowledge of the new

machinery of the industrial revolution to the United States in 1789.

With its focus on individual liberties and economic free enterprise, the United States industrialized rapidly, and within a century it had used its vast spaces and rich natural resources to become the most technologically advanced nation in the world.

The United States rapidly expanded its territory westward, mostly by purchase rather than by conquest. President Thomas Jefferson purchased the Louisiana Territory, including most of the land between the Mississippi River and the Rocky Mountains, by paying $15 million to Spain. The United States bought Florida from Spain in 1819 for another $5 million dollars.

The United States absorbed Texas after the Texans revolted against Mexico in 1845 and went on to defeat Mexico in a war that brought much of California and the Southwest into the United States. A settlement with Great Britain brought in the northwestern portion of the nation, and by 1853 the borders of the United States with Canada and Mexico were the same as they are today.

During the Napoleonic Wars that took place between 1796 and 1815, the United States attempted to remain neutral but found itself at war with Great Britain once again, beginning in 1812. Even though the British burned Washington, the United States survived the war, ironically winning the climactic Battle of New Orleans in January 1815, after the formal peace treaty had been signed.

War of 1812 between England and United States

Thanks in part to the chaos in Europe during the Napoleonic Wars, the Latin American colonies to the south of the United States began to break away from Spain and Portugal. In 1823, the United States declared the Western Hemisphere to be closed to European territorial exploitation and guaranteed the continued freedom of the Latin Americans nations. This Monroe Doctrine, advanced during the presidency of James Monroe (1758–1831), represented one of the first assertions of the new American power in the world.

During this entire period, the institution of slavery continued to be a divisive force in America. Half the states were free and half allowed slavery, but the free states of the North were more populous and industrialized. Many Northerners considered slavery immoral and at odds with the American ideals stated in the Declaration of Independence and the Constitution. Southerners felt threatened by the North and did not want to give up a way of life that was based on the institution of slavery.

U.S. Civil War begins

As westward expansion continued, the issue became acute. As each new state was admitted to the Union, it had to be decided if it would be slave or free. Eventually, the political leaders of the country ran out of compromises and the nation plunged into a civil war.

Abraham Lincoln, elected as the presidential candidate of the new Republican party, never wavered from his devotion to restoring the Union, which had been sundered when thirteen Southern states seceded to form the Confederate States of America.

U.S. Civil War ends

Lincoln was assassinated on April 14, 1865, only days after the victory of the Union forces ended the war, but he succeeded in his mission and is remembered today as one of the greatest of American presidents.

Some of the slaves were freed even before the war ended, but the struggle of black people for their civil rights continued for well over another one hundred years, and the issue of race relations remains a major force for destabilization in the United States even today.

After the Civil War, the United States felt itself comfortably isolated from the rest of the world by the Atlantic and Pacific oceans. The country's considerable energies could now be turned to developing the western frontier. Many of the Native American tribes fought ferociously against the incursions of settlers and soldiers onto their sacred lands. In many ways, it was a replay of the old struggle between the civilization built around farms and cities and the hunter/herder tribal life.

The Indians acquitted themselves well, but they were overwhelmed by superior technology and numbers. By 1890, most of them had been restricted to reservations.

The United States bought Alaska from Russia in 1867 for $7.2 billion. Like the earlier Louisiana Purchase, the Alaska deal was initially criticized, but later became a new frontier of great value to the United States.

For a long time, the drive of the United States to develop its own territory kept it from competing with European nations for overseas possessions. However, the Spanish-American war in 1898 led to the annexation of Puerto Rico and the Philippines, which had been Spanish colonies. The Hawaiian Islands were also annexed in that year, and the United States began to taste imperialist power in a small way.

For the next one hundred years, the United States oscillated between isolation and involvement in world affairs. Its power made intervention possible, and its sometimes messianic commitment to certain political ideals made intervention seem palatable. At the same time, people had come to the New World to escape the corruption they saw in European societies, and President George Washington, in his farewell address, had warned the nation against "foreign entanglements."

American isolation was shattered first by World War I. The United States managed to stay neutral until 1917, even though most Americans sided with the British and French against Germany. The German policy of using submarines to sink ships in the Atlantic, including American ships, finally brought the United States into the war.

American involvement came late in this so-called "war to end all wars," but did help to tip the balance against the exhausted Germans, who were forced to surrender in 1918.

World War I devastated Europe but had left the United States almost untouched, and the United States emerged as the richest nation in the world. It was the world's great creditor nation, since it had lent money to the British and French and could now expect to get it back.

However, the European nations were unable to repay the loans, leading most Americans to feel cheated, and supporting the urge to be isolated from Europe's quarrels once again. The United States therefore refused to join the League of Nations, which had been set up after World War I, even though the American president, Woodrow Wilson (1856–1924) had initiated the process that led to its formation.

American absence weakened the League as a peace-keeping device, and American isolationism removed what might have been a strong hand preventing the rise of one of the strongest antidemocratic movements ever known—fascism.

Fascism spread rapidly after the Great Depression, beginning in 1929, led to impoverishment and deep insecurity, especially in defeated countries such as Germany. Millions of people began to search for strong leaders who would take them out of the quagmire, even at the cost of their liberty.

Benito Mussolini (1883–1945), formerly a Socialist, came to power as a fascist dictator in Italy in 1922. Adolf Hitler (1889–1945) was actually elected to be the leader of the German Weimar Republic in 1933. The civil war in Spain produced a fascist government under Francisco Franco (1892–1975), who was helped in his fight by Mussolini and Hitler.

Fascism presented itself as a bulwark against Communism, which appealed to many in Great Britain, France, and even the United States, where people sometimes argued that fascism was the lesser of the two evils. The dictators used clever propaganda to soften opposition to their aggression and oppression. Mussolini harked back to the glory of the old Roman Empire to inspire Italians to support him, and Hitler made it clear that he did not want to go to war with Great Britain and the United States.

The people of the western democracies, having suffered a devastating war only twenty years before, wanted to try every possible avenue to avoid war. This led to a policy of appeasement, giving in to Hitler in exchange for his guarantees that each demand would be the last.

World War II begins with German invasion of Poland Eventually, Hitler's invasion of Poland in 1939 triggered declarations of war by England and France, because of their treaty commitments to the Poles. By 1941, Hitler controlled all of Europe except Great Britain. It appeared that he might realize his goal of world conquest, but then he showed himself not to be a superman, just another follower of the inevitably disastrous imperial path.

Once Hitler invaded the Soviet Union, his fate, like that of Napoleon, was sealed. In addition, the Japanese attack on Pearl Harbor during the same year brought the United States into the war, ensuring that the Allies would have sufficient power to win, even though the process took another four years.

Germany invades Soviet Union

Japan attacks United States at Pearl Harbor

After World War II, Europe was once again prostrate, and the United States was once again largely untouched, so that American power dominated the world more than ever. The United States alone possessed the atomic bomb, and people began to speak of the American Century and the Pax Americana.

World War II ends

American isolationism was dealt a severe blow by World War II. American postwar policy tended more toward being "the policeman of the world," helping friendly governments and opposing enemies. The Soviet Union, a wartime ally, became a postwar competitor. The Soviets had taken over eastern Europe and seemed intent on promoting Communism around the world. The danger to the United States increased markedly when the Soviet Union developed its own nuclear weapons in 1949, replacing the "balance of power" with a "balance of terror."

It was impossible for the United States and the Soviet Union to go to war, because nuclear weapons guaranteed "mutual assured destruction" (MAD). Therefore, the struggle between the two powers took place by proxy in the Third World countries. The United States sent American forces to Asia twice to fight Communist armies directly. The Korean War, which began when North Korea invaded South Korea in 1950, eventually involved the Chinese and ended in a frustrating stalemate. The war in Vietnam, which involved an effort to assist the South Vietnamese government against the North Vietnamese and internal forces known as the National Liberation Front, ended with American withdrawal in the early 1970s, and the defeat of the South Vietnamese in 1975.

Korean War begins

War in Vietnam ends

The war in Vietnam grew out of the American policy of containing Communism wherever it appeared, a policy that did seem to work in regard to the Soviet Union in Europe, but was less successful in other areas of the world. American involvement escalated from a small contingent of advisers to a force that included almost half a million men, and involved constant bombing of North Vietnam.

The war lasted too long without visible progress toward any attainable goals, and proved that the will of the people must be strongly united for a democracy to win a war. President Richard Nixon, who was elected in 1968 with a promise that he had a "secret plan" to end the war, did preside over American withdrawal from Vietnam. His resignation over the Watergate Scandal led ultimately to the election of President Jimmy Carter, who was much less inclined to involve the United States directly in overseas interventions.

By the 1980s, the superpower competition between the United States and the Soviet Union had become focused on a mixture of covert actions and a race to develop new technologies that would give one side or the other a strategic advantage.

Neil Armstrong first man on the moon

The United States had already shown its muscle in a race involving high technology when it challenged the Soviet Union to a moon race and won, even though the Soviets insisted they had never agreed to the race in the first place.

When President Ronald Reagan came into office in 1980, he seemed intent upon stoking the fires of competition with the Soviet Union once again, calling them the "evil empire," and making commitments to help "freedom fighters" resist Communism around the world. In 1983, he also announced that the United States would undertake a strategic defense initiative, putting a defensive shield in outer space that would make nuclear weapons obsolete.

As the decade of the 1980s drew to a close, it was much too early to know whether it was American policy or internal Soviet conditions that caused a dramatic change in the Soviet Union's policies. However, that decade ended with great hope for lessened world tensions, as the Soviets loosened their grip on eastern Europe and began to enter into serious arms control talks with the United States.

At the same time, calls for democracy reached a virtual fever pitch around the world, from East Germany to Mongolia, from Hungary to Nepal. Suddenly, it seemed that the peoples of the world were finally casting their ballots, and it was not for those in the mold of Attila the Hun, but for those who modeled themselves after Solon and Pericles.

WHEN WE FIRST BEGAN OUR SURVEY OF THE EVOLUTION OF civilization over the millennia, it was possible to talk about the world as one entity, millennium by millennium. There were few humans on the earth, their impact was relatively small, and we did not have much knowledge about them. As we approached our own millennium, however, it was necessary to make our analysis region by region, because there were now many civilizations and so much to describe in each one. Indeed, as we moved closer to the present, it became clear that we could only give cursory attention to each region.

The World As One

However, as we look ahead to the time beyond 2000, something remarkable has occurred—we can once again view the world as one. Even though separate nations and civilizations continue to exist, there is a growing awareness of the earth as one system in which everyone on the planet is connected to everyone else.

This awareness is due largely to technological development, which has been the driving force in human history during this millennium and especially in the past century. Space travel has contributed to the change by giving us our first clear picture of the whole earth from space, back in the 1960s. Communications satellites continuously reinforce the new perspective, providing us with the ability to instantaneously communicate from any point on the planet to any other point.

Sputnik launched; first artificial satellite

Yuri Gagaran first man in space

Because of the worldwide technological infrastructure, including telephones, computers, television, radio, and airplanes, humans have become aware not only of what is happening everywhere but also how it affects others who may be thousands of miles away. A good example of the shift can be seen in growing ecological awareness, which was minuscule in the 1960s, but has now become a worldwide concern in the 1990s.

First "Earth Day"

The change can also be seen in how rapidly ideas, such as

democracy, spread around the world "infecting" entire populations and moving them to revolutionary actions. After eleven thousand years in which emperors and generals tried to unify the world through force, it has now been done—to a large extent, peacefully. From its minuscule beginnings in the Tigris-Euphrates Valley and along the Nile, human civilization now dominates the planet, and humans hold the key to futher evolution on Earth.

As we look ahead it seems clear that humans are beginning to realize that the future of humanity and all the other life-forms on Earth cannot be understood only in terms of the needs of a few individuals or nation-states. The future must be understood in terms of the needs of the planet as a whole, including all the different systems that keep Earth intact and evolving.

Perhaps humans have learned, too, that in each millennium of the past, all the struggles between people and nations for power often paled in the face of a single achievement of the human mind—the invention of the alphabet, the development of a new philosophy, the creation of a better political system, or the construction of a new cosmology.

Could it be that the human mind is ultimately more powerful than the armies and navies that have roamed restlessly across the planet, trying to impose the will of some political figure on others? If so, it becomes fascinating to ask, What problems are confronted by the human mind and human civilization in the next millennium, and how will we go about meeting those challenges?

CHAPTER SEVEN

THE NEXT MILLENNIUM

BEYOND A.D. 2000

HAVING FOLLOWED CIVILIZATION FROM ITS BEGINNINGS TO the present, a millennium at a time, it is now our task to look beyond 2000 and get a glimpse of what life might be like between 2000 and 3000.

The task is, of course, impossible for two reasons.

First, the future is not graven in stone. It is not an ineluctable Fate that cannot be avoided or affected by human actions. We choose our own future by our behavior in the present, and we can decide to start a nuclear war or make peace instead. We can decide to poison Earth or heat it until it becomes uninhabitable. We may also avoid these futures by deciding on specific courses of action, and there is no way that we can predict what the human community will choose to do.

Second, there are unpredictable events that change everything and don't involve conscious decisions. What if China had had a series of emperors, all of whom were fascinated by exploration in the early 1400s? What if the Roman Empire had developed an equitable method of taxation? What if Genghis Khan had died young and there had never been a Mongol Empire, across which hints concerning printing and the magnetic compass and gunpowder could have reached western Europe in the 1200s?

There are so many "what ifs." What if Columbus's ships had run into a storm and had been sunk, so that he never returned from his voyage to report on the discovery of the New World? Closer to the present time, what if Mikhail Gorbachev had failed to become the leader of the Soviet Union?

There will be unpredictable future events that make the most sober and logical estimates of future trends turn out to be so ridiculously wrong that anyone reading them a hundred years from now will have to laugh.

Nevertheless, our review of the past has certainly revealed a few patterns that seem to appear and reappear frequently, pointing in the direction we should look as we peer into the future. Looking back at previous millennia, we are struck at first by the enormous changes that have taken place, but there are other trends that have been fairly constant over time.

We can try to pick out some events that look as though they *will* or *might* come to pass, and consider how that will affect what is to come. Let us look, then, at some of the key factors that seem certain to have a major impact on the next millennium.

Population

ONE OF THE BASIC THEMES OF HUMAN EXISTENCE ON Earth over the millennia has been the continuing growth in population. However, something extraordinary has happened in the past millennium, making population growth a trend that cannot be ignored as we look ahead.

We do not really know the world population in the past. Taking accurate censuses over large areas of the earth is a relatively recent development, and even today we must estimate the actual population of the earth. However, the best estimates suggest that the advance of human population from the beginning of civilization until now, counting by the millennial years, looks something like this:

Year	Estimated Population	Percent Increase
8000 B.C.	4 million	—
7000 B.C.	4.3 million	7.5
6000 B.C.	4.6 million	6.5
5000 B.C.	5 million	8.7

Year	Estimated Population	Percent Increase
4000 B.C.	7 million	40
3000 B.C.	14 million	100
2000 B.C.	27 million	93
1000 B.C.	50 million	85
1 B.C.	170 million	240
A.D. 1000	265 million	56
A.D. 2000	6000 million	2165

Until now, the population has always increased, but it actually has grown relatively slowly. For the first three thousand years of civilization, the population grew less than 10 percent per millennium as the invention of agriculture spread outward very slowly and the food supply increased modestly.

After 6000 B.C., the population began to double roughly every millennium, as agriculture spread out more rapidly. However, in the past thousand years, the population has increased something like twenty-two times—a dramatic change from previous years.

What happened? For one thing, an unpredictable event intervened. The age of exploration meant that western Europeans discovered the Americas, South Africa, and Australia. They poured into these nonagricultural areas and agriculturalized them. This, as we already know, is the first step in establishing civilization as we know it. Russia also expanded eastward, putting larger and larger areas under cultivation. As we have also seen, population expands when agriculture increases, and so it has.

Population has even grown in densely populated areas, such as India and China, as people learned to farm more intensely and make use of every corner of the land.

Even more instructive is the fact that the growth in population in this most recent millennium was not even. From 1000 to 1800, the population increased from 320 million to 900 million, a growth of 2.8 times. That is not really very much more than the millennial increases that preceded it. *Popularly considered first year of new decade, century, and millennium*

However, from 1800 to 2000, the population increased from 900 million to 6 billion, or 6.6 times in a mere two centuries. It *Estimated world population at 6 billion plus*

900 million to 6 billion, or 6.6 times in a mere two centuries. It is truly accurate to say that we are living in a population explosion.

Population growth is understandable, but why has this explosion taken place? The answer is that in the 1800s, the industrial revolution built upon the foundations of the agricultural transformation that had begun thousands of years before. Power machinery was applied to agriculture, dramatically increasing food supply. Chemical fertilizers, new irrigation systems, and improved strains of plants were developed and further increased the food supply. All of these developments acted to reduce the number of people who died of famine.

To us, famine is an anomaly, a catastrophe to be avoided or mitigated. From a human point of view, this is true, and it is a noble cause to attempt to reduce or eliminate hunger on a global basis. However, within the natural world, famine is also a mechanism that keeps any species from growing beyond the ability of the environment to support it.

Disease is another killer that humans learned to control to a great extent during the past few centuries. We can prevent or cure many infectious diseases, operate to correct life-threatening problems, and we have learned techniques for improving lifestyles that lengthen life itself. Thus, the death rate from disease, contagious and degenerative, has gone down, *and* that lower rate is now applied to a much larger population.

Finally, improved living conditions not only lower the death rate, but can also elevate the birth rate. This is not always true, because it has been found that the birth rate actually drops in industrialized countries. This is so because large families are not needed to help run farms, as nations mechanize agriculture and become industrial. They no longer choose to have more children to care for them in their old age, a common practice in less wealthy countries.

Nevertheless, better health clearly reduces infant mortality, thereby allowing more children to survive the early months and years and grow into adults who will in turn live longer.

Taken together, all of these factors help to explain the population explosion. It may seem as if the explosion is a good thing, proving that we are in better control of our lives and our environment.

Perhaps this is true to some extent, but it cannot continue. Let us assume that the human species is perfectly willing to increase its numbers by 6.6 times in two centuries, as it did in the past 200 years, with a rate of increase even faster in the last half century. If this rate continued into the next millennium, the population of the earth would be about 75 trillion people in the year 3000. It is clearly impossible for the earth to support so vast a number of human beings, or even a small fraction of it.

Of course, we might argue that the earth will not be the only home of human beings by the year 3000, and this is probably true. We will most likely be sending colonists to the moon or to Mars, and we will even build brand new worlds capable of holding thousands or millions of people each.

Still, at the present time, the population of Earth is increasing at the rate of 70 million people per year. We must ask, When can we look forward to the capacity of sending 70 million people per year to live in space? Even the most optimistic advocates of space settlement do not believe that we can do it in the near future.

Even if we did manage to send so many human beings off-planet, those people will continue to multiply and compete for new homes with additional people sent out from Earth. Again, most scenarios assume that human beings will be focused on developing the Solar System in the next few hundred years, and while it is vast, it is not infinite. Even the Solar System cannot hold an unlimited number of people.

In addition, it is obvious from simple calculations that, at the present rate of increase, the total mass of human flesh and blood in the universe would equal the total mass of the universe itself by the year 9000—and then we would simply run out of universe into which we could expand.

It follows, then, that the rate of human increase must be reduced right here on Earth and right now. It must also be brought down to zero growth, or if the increase continues much longer, to negative growth. One of the great problems facing humanity in our post-2000 world, is to achieve this goal.

There are only two ways in which a population increase can be reduced and/or stopped. One is to have the death rate rise until it is higher than the birth rate. The other is to have the birth rate fall until it is lower than the death rate.

The former, as has already been pointed out, is the natural method of population control. Any species will experience a population explosion in a period when food is plentiful and predators are scarce. Then, however, there comes the time of sparse food and plentiful predators, and a period of terrible hardship and death.

If the population problem is left to itself, something like this will happen to humanity. Indeed, it is already happening in certain regions of the world. Ultimately, the population will not rise to 75 trillion. Instead, there will be periods of increasing famine, of disease striking at hunger-weakened bodies, more violent deaths as people scramble for what food they can find. The death rate will go up and up in a horrifying progression.

Here we have the Four Horsemen of the Apocalypse, described in the biblical book of Revelation: famine, disease, war, and death. Such a scenario is catastrophic, however, and would surely wipe out our complex civilization that has been agonizingly developed over the previous millennia. We would be reduced to remnants of a once great culture living in the equivalent of the Stone Age. No one can possibly desire a solution of this type.

That leaves us with a drop in the birth rate as the only possible way of expecting to reach the year 3000 living in relative peace and prosperity. How is this to be achieved, then?

First, people must *want* to have fewer babies. There has been a drive throughout history to have as many babies as possible. Infant mortality was high, life expectancy was low, and a crowd of babies was the only insurance that some would live to have babies of their own. As we have noted, in poor countries without social welfare, many children would ensure that the parents would have care in their old age.

To be sure, we have long since passed the stage where a

plethora of babies is required, and we have reached the point where too many babies will be fatal. However, old habits, old points of view, and strong traditions die hard. In addition, there are influential voices in the world who oppose birth control on religious grounds, and encourage large families even today. This, too, has a powerful effect on the behavior of people.

Where many babies are required, the social status of women tends to be low. Since they must have one baby after another, it is difficult (or impossible) for them to get an education, and they have no time to play a role in the world outside the home. Even today, in those societies in which the social status of women is low, the birth rate is high, or vice versa. Moreover, if women are kept out of participation in the mainstream, parenting becomes almost the only way in which they can emphasize their importance and social status.

It follows that in a society in which women are treated as social, economic, and political equals, the birth rate will automatically drop. Women who want to have a career find that this goal must be balanced with parenting, and that it becomes very difficult with many children. In addition, men must become more involved in the parenting process, taking time away from economic activity on their part. This is another reason that, in industrialized societies, birth rates drop—given a certain amount of income (even with two people working), increasing the number of family members means that the family's overall standard of living must fall.

It is for all these reasons that most of the population increase is taking place in the so-called Third World, where old traditions are strong, the social status of women is not very high, and the standard of living is already low, so that increasing the number of family members may not have as noticeable an impact. Unfortunately, it is in the Third World that the increases cannot easily be absorbed.

Therefore, we may look forward to a beyond-2000 world in which some form of economic development takes place more evenly on a global basis, and women take their rightful place in

Population growth reaches equilibrium

society. We can be somewhat confident that this will happen, because otherwise, it seems that our civilization will not survive.

Even if people do not want to have more babies, how can that be brought about? Partial or complete abstention is, of course, one way to ensure that fewer children will be born, and humans have gone through many cycles of being more liberal and then more conservative about sexual practices. Sometimes, this is out of choice, as in the case of priests. In other cases, there are social conventions that encourage abstention, such as the idea that people should not have extramarital sex. Today, there are great changes in sexual behavior born out of the fear of contracting a disease such as AIDS.

It seems highly unlikely, however, that abstention alone will be sufficient to damp down the human population explosion in the next millennium. If current trends continue, we can expect that there will instead be a further decoupling of sex and child-bearing. While contraception is still opposed by many, it is accepted by others as an alternative to abortion, infanticide, and child abandonment. Contraception also lends itself to the unique human quality of inventively using technology to deal with social problems, and for that reason the importance of contraception is likely to increase in the next millennium.

Energy

WE ALREADY KNOW THAT HOW HUMAN BEINGS UTILIZE energy is a critical variable in how civilization develops. Indeed, the ability to control energy, whether it be making wood fires or building power plants, is a prerequisite of civilization.

The population issue and the energy variable are also intimately linked. The danger of overpopulation is not merely that there are too many people in too small a space. Each additional human being requires a supply of food, some kind of shelter, a degree of security, and a way of disposing of wastes.

Human beings need far more space than the ground on which they stand. They need farms, mines, houses and structures of all kinds, to say nothing of roads, bridges, and the appurtenances of transportation and communication. Even in relatively primitive societies, the room required for expanding societies means that forests must be cut down for firewood and to clear the ground for farms. Industrialized societies require even more room, because the components of civilization are larger and more complex.

The human need for so much room is bad news for other forms of life. From the very beginning, humans have hunted down other life-forms, without much thought to the possibility of extinction. Mammoths and other large creatures of the ice ages were very likely driven to extinction by precivilized hunters. Now, civilization, with all its new weapons, has even brought all the other great predators to the edge of disappearance.

Even when human beings do not want to destroy other life-forms, the mere fact that they need so much room wipes out the living space, or ecological niches for these other creatures. At the present time, therefore, despite all that many people are doing to preserve life, the rate of extinction is extraordinarily high.

This means that we are severely damaging the ecological balance of our planet, to our peril. All life is interdependent, and we cannot wipe out species after species without affecting ourselves adversely.

Civilization has always produced harmful effects on the planet itself. Agriculture, for all its benefits to humans, tends to damage the soil, for example. Irrigation has drawn too heavily on the water table, and has brought in salt water that ruins the crops. Herding has multiplied the number of grazing and browsing animals, who have destroyed vegetation and converted fertile areas into semi-deserts.

Prior to the industrialization of the planet, however, human beings were not able to do too much damage to the ecosystem. It is since industrialization and the copious use of energy at a much greater rate than ever before that damaging effects have gone into high gear.

Ordinary wastes such as biological excretions or garbage, slowly rot and reenter the biological cycle, thereby being used over and over again. We consume oxygen and produce carbon dioxide, while plants consume the carbon dioxide and produce oxygen again. Animal wastes fertilize plants and serve as food for some insects and bacteria, and such wastes are eventually converted into forms that can once again be used as foods.

The new industrial processes, however, produce wastes that are not a part of the natural world. Plastics, for example, accumulate in dumps and are not broken down and recycled—throwaway diapers are now accumulating at a high rate, and their convenience to busy parents is being balanced by their harm to the ecosystem.

Many industrial waste products are actively toxic, so that air, water, and soil are being poisoned. As a result, other forms of life are dying out.

In theory, all the problems can be corrected, but it can only be done by the expenditure of energy, and by taking a close look at how we use energy. It seems clear that the agenda of the next millennium will necessarily include energy as a high priority item.

To solve the problem, however, we must understand it fully. Originally, human beings had only the energy of their own muscles and those of animals at their disposal. They learned to make use of the inanimate energy of wind and running water, but wind was erratic and running water was confined to only a few sites.

The use of fire supplied energy, of course, but it was not until the invention of the steam engine that the energy of fire could be harnessed in a massive and versatile fashion. With the industrial revolution came the real "age of energy."

Almost all the energy used in industrial societies is obtained by the combination of carbon and hydrogen atoms in fuels of various kinds with the oxygen of the atmosphere. The first fuel was wood, with a minor addition of animal fats, plant oils, and waxes. With the industrial revolution, coal, oil, and natural gas came into use. These are the products of life-forms that dwelt hundreds of millions of years ago and are lumped together as fossil fuels.

The burning of these fuels has major disadvantages, starting with irritation caused by smoke. At first, it was enough to direct the smoke through a chimney into the air at the top of a structure, but there are so many fires constantly burning now that the earth's atmosphere is becoming unbearably filthy.

Impurities in coal and oil introduce oxides of sulfur and nitrogen into the atmosphere and ozone. All of these are actively toxic and place a serious strain on human lungs. They also dissolve in falling water to produce the acid rain that is destroying forests and lakes. The exhaust of countless automobiles is a major contributor to this ongoing air pollution.

Coal and oil also produce carbon dioxide, which is poured into the atmosphere faster than plant life can withdraw it again. This problem is compounded because the forests most efficient at removing carbon dioxide are being cut down. A small amount of carbon dioxide in the atmosphere is essential to plant life and therefore to animals. So far, even though human beings are pouring millions of tons of carbon dioxide into the atmosphere, the main problem is not its effect on breathing.

However, carbon dioxide, while transparent to ordinary light, absorbs infrared radiation. Light from the sun reaches the earth, but the planet must get rid of that energy at night, re-radiating it into space as infrared energy. The carbon dioxide interferes with that process, and the earth gets slightly warmer than it otherwise would be. This is called the greenhouse effect.

The small-scale greenhouse effect produced by the carbon dioxide that is naturally present in the air keeps the earth from being in a perpetual ice age. However, the additional carbon dioxide now entering the atmosphere will make the earth warmer, and alter its climate for the worse.

If we are going to reach the year 3000 safely, we are going to have to find new sources of energy. Natural gas is the cleanest of the fossil fuels, and is the least likely to pollute the atmosphere. However, it still produces carbon dioxide and adds to the greenhouse effect. Besides, even if we somehow were to learn how to remove the carbon dioxide from the atmosphere as fast as it enters, the fossil fuels exist only in limited quantity, and the oil and natural gas will not last long past A.D. 2000. Coal might last until 3000, but not far beyond that time.

We need energy sources that are nonpolluting and that will also last for thousands of years. In the 1940s and 1950s, many believed that nuclear fission would be the answer to our concerns. However, building and operating nuclear power plants has proven to be more expensive than expected, and the dangers of nuclear power cannot be minimized. Even if the plants operate with perfect safety, we are still confronted with the problem of how to dispose of the radioactive wastes they produce. In addition, the Three-Mile Island accident in the United States and the Chernobyl explosion in the Soviet Union shows that accidents do happen, with traumatic consequences.

The public has now become extremely uneasy about nuclear fission and its potential for disaster, and it is unlikely that this form of energy will be readily accepted as a major solution in the next millennium.

Beyond nuclear fission, there are two other significant possibilities. One is nuclear fusion, which produces more energy than nuclear fission and uses heavy hydrogen as a principal material. Fusion's ability to outperform fission is encouraging, as is the fact that there is enough heavy hydrogen available to supply Earth with ample energy for the rest of our planet's lifetime. In theory, nuclear fusion will also produce far less dangerous radiation than nuclear fission does.

The problem with fusion is uncertainty. To date, a lot of money has been spent on fusion research, without any result pointing to its use on a massive scale. Part of the problem is that fusion is caused by actually fusing atoms together, something that in itself requires large amounts of heat and energy. In fact, the only way that a hydrogen bomb (fusion-based) can be detonated is to explode an atomic bomb (fission-based) next to it.

Recently, some scientists reported that they had perfected a low-cost means of producing cold fusion. In other words, they were producing energy derived from fusion, but without the energy that everyone thought would be necessary to succeed in the experiment. At first, many people were very excited about the announcement, but as time went on members of the scientific community grew increasingly skeptical about these claims.

The situation may change—an unpredictable event may well intervene, and the energy problem will be resolved by cold fusion or something like it. However, as we move toward the year 2000, there is no guarantee that fusion is any more a solution to the energy crisis than is fission.

A second approach is to search for ways to better utilize the energy of the sun (solar energy) directly. Unlike coal and oil, solar energy is nonpolluting and does not produce wastes as fission does. Also, unlike fusion, we do know how to use solar energy, and it is actually being utilized on a modest scale.

However, to use solar energy more effectively on a global basis we would need to create vast arrays of photoelectric cells to collect the sunlight, and these are not yet cheap enough or efficient enough to do the job properly.

It has been proposed that satellites can be put into orbit to collect sunlight in space itself. The solar energy would then be converted to microwaves and beamed down to Earth for redistribution here. Concerns have been raised about the environmental dangers of sending microwave energy through the atmosphere, and we would still have to build large fields of cells to collect the energy. However, solar power satellites remain an intriguing possibility for resolving our energy dilemma.

There are many other possible sources of energy, such as the tides, wave action, the earth's own internal heat, and even wind power. All of these hold out the hope that they can make a nondestructive contribution to our energy needs.

Energy will remain on the human agenda in the next millen- *New energy sources* nium, and we cannot foresee how it will be resolved. The solution *developed* will most likely involve a mixed approach, including many different sources of energy, always striving for the best results with the least environmental damage. It seems improbable that the next millennium will see humanity returning to a preindustrial, tribal lifestyle with low energy requirements. At the same time, our environmental consciousness is extremely high, and pressures to protect the earth are certain to increase over time.

For all of these reasons, we can expect that the next millennium will be a time when humans learn how to evolve our civilization without destroying our planet in the process.

War

CAN HUMANITY HOPE TO SOLVE THE ENORMOUS PROBLEMS posed by an ever-worsening population and the deleterious results of our energy consumption if the nations of Earth concentrate on fighting one another? It hardly seems likely, but will nations change their behavior in time?

There are those who would say that human beings have fought one another throughout history and there is no way of stopping them from doing so. This book's review of the millennia certainly might be interpreted to support that point of view. From 8000 B.C. to just before A.D. 2000, human history often appears to be a swirl of power struggles, as one political leader after another tries to gain advantage over competitors.

While this is part of the human story, however, it should be seen as only one part. During the same period, other trends have also developed that are more encouraging.

All through history there have been two ways whereby a society could improve itself beyond what it could do by its own muscles and minds. One path of improvement comes through trading with another society, giving up something of which you have a surplus for something that you lack. Through trade and business, all societies can improve their way of life.

Specialized resources available to one group and not another, and special abilities developed by one group and not another, can be spread out. In this way, each society has to some extent the benefits of all the resources and ingenuity in the world.

The other path to improvement is to move in on a richer but weaker society and simply appropriate its property by force. This is a pattern that appears with great frequency in human history, most often in the struggle between the "barbarians" on an empire's periphery and the more civilized subjects of the empire itself.

In essence, then, a society bent on improving its lot can choose between business and war. War appears all too often the method of choice, especially when one society lacks what another society wants. Lacking the wherewithal for trade, war may appear to be the only way out. Besides, war is faster, and may seem to be cheaper. After all, you can take *everything*, giving up nothing of your own. To some people, war is also more exciting and seems more honorable than commercial activities.

However, war is necessarily destructive, and a victor taking over a defeated civilization soon discovers that the benefits are only short-term unless he can keep that civilization going. What happens, usually, is that the victor adopts civilized ways, but becomes an aristocracy ruling over a defeated (and rebellious) peasantry.

As long as war produced a limited amount of destruction that could be set right without too much effort, it might be made to seem a profitable activity. In general, however, war has become steadily more destructive, while societies have become increasingly complex. As a result, it is far more difficult to restore a society to something approaching normalcy after it has been overcome.

In the 1800s, Prussia fought a series of short wars that helped make it the temporary leader of Europe, transforming itself into Germany at the same time. In that era, the balance between war and commerce was such that war might still be used effectively to achieve a state's goals.

Even World War II, the most destructive war ever fought, did not push the defeated nations to a condition beyond recovery. The United States, the relatively unscathed victor, helped restore a devastated Western Europe, and Japan (which had even gone through the horror of nuclear attack).

However, once nuclear weapons were invented, no one could ignore the fact that full-scale war would push civilizations back to a state perhaps even more primitive than conditions in 8000 B.C. If the two superpowers of the twentieth century—the United States and Soviet Union—unleashed their nuclear arsenals, not only would they be destroyed, but a blanket of radioactive fallout would cover the world. No one could escape the effects of such a war, any more than the dinosaurs could avoid the impact of the comet that supposedly hit the earth 26 million years ago.

Under the circumstances, all-out wars simply cannot be fought any more, and the governments of all the major powers know it. Since 1945, there have been a number of minor wars between nonnuclear powers, and even the Soviet Union and United States have engaged in these fights. In 1962, the entire world teetered on the brink of nuclear destruction with the Cuban Missile Crisis, but everyone backed away from it, perhaps fully realizing the implications of a nuclear world for the first time.

The United States learned in Vietnam and the Soviet Union learned in Afghanistan that these kinds of wars are hardly worth the price to be paid for fighting them. Less-developed nations will still fight one another or carry on civil wars over long periods, but one must be insane to think that they serve any purpose. Eight years of fighting between Iran and Iraq, for example, ended inconclusively, but with a horrific loss of life. The civil war in Lebanon has (at this writing) lasted twice as long, with the same result. In Northern Ireland, internecine strife seems to be endless, but also without useful results for the people who live there.

The new conditions produce ironic results. Nations that consider themselves natural enemies, just as, say, the Spartans and Athenians once did, can no longer act directly on their hostility. The Soviet Union and the United States, who have been engaged in an intense cold war for some forty years, have never struck at each other in anger, or even broken off diplomatic relations. Not only do they not dare fight each other, they don't even dare to stop talking with each other.

As the year 2000 approaches, tensions between the superpowers are easing, and the cold war seems to be ending. Is this the end of war itself on the planet Earth or just the beginning of the end? The answer to this question depends, to some extent, on how successful the other path to improvement—commerce—turns out to be.

What, then, about the other side of the coin? If war seems less useful to nations in achieving their goals, does business seem to be more useful? The answer is clearly, yes. The two nations, Japan and Germany, who were most devastated by World War II, were also forbidden to engage in warlike activities. Japan was even prevented from developing an army, and Germany was divided in two.

As part of the Communist bloc, East Germany was not able to engage fully in business activities for some time, but Japan and West Germany had no choice but to focus on business as their way of achieving influence in the world. The results have been remarkable, as these two countries have become highly prosperous economic superpowers.

In addition, as we approach the next millennium, business has become completely multinational, and people have grown accustomed to the fact that the economy of each nation is affected by the economy of other nations. As a result, cooperation rather than conflict is clearly the order of the day. The advanced industrial powers meet annually to plan their economies, and western Europe plans to create a continent-wide economic union in 1992.

Moreover, the Communist nations are rapidly abandoning Communism and centralized state planning, seeking to reintegrate themselves into the world economy. They are doing so, not because of having been defeated in war, but because they see that this is the path providing them with the greatest long-term advantage.

500th anniversary of Columbus' voyage

International Space Year

Thus, while the abolition of war is an altruistic goal for many who are working toward that end, nation-states act in terms of their self-interest, and war will be abolished because nations no longer see the use of force to be a tool for advancing themselves.

As economic cooperation increases on a global basis, it appears inevitable that political connections will also intensify. In Europe, for example, the focus has been on economic issues for some forty years, but political unity has been served by these developments, as well. The European Parliament has now evolved from an institution with relatively little power to an organization with real influence. Perhaps the European Parliament is a harbinger of things to come on a global scale.

It is clear, then, that in our passage from 2000 to 3000, the nature of the global problems humanity faces, coupled with the obvious advantages an interlocking world economic system offers,

War declines as means of settling disputes

will abolish war. These trends will also lead to an ever-closer cooperation among nations, although each may be willing and even eager to keep its own culture intact. In fact, a variety of cultures within a cooperating world is to be desired. It will make human life more interesting and encourage the forces of creativity and art.

Ecological balance is achieved

However, we must be realistic and ask ourselves, Can we seriously expect that the hatreds and suspicions that have built up for millennia can be done away with, or sublimated in some way? The answer may be yes, at least to the extent of building a cooperative world community.

To see how this might come about, let's take a look at the next trend.

Space Exploration

AS OUR MILLENNIAL REVIEW HAS SHOWN, HUMAN BEINGS have always engaged in monumental projects. The ancient Egyptians turned the Nile River delta into a garden and built the pyramids with little more than their own muscle power. Columbus sailed the Atlantic Ocean in three small ships and discovered a New World. In two centuries, western Europe had industrialized itself and the entire planet.

Yet perhaps the most breathtaking feat thus far performed by human beings was launching themselves into space and reaching the moon. Between 1969 and 1972, six American expeditions reached the moon, and twelve men walked its surface. Project Apollo pulled together the resources of an entire nation to accomplish something that no one knew how to do—put a human being on the moon and bring him back safely. The most astounding aspect of this accomplishment is that it was done in only eight years!

Of course, human space exploration has included many activities other than Apollo. Since the space age began with the Soviet Union's launching of the Sputnik satellite in 1957, we have explored much of the Solar System with unmanned probes, sent numerous satellites into Earth's orbit, and built manned space stations in orbit as well.

For all that has been accomplished in space exploration, much more could have been done. The pace of development is not limited by technological knowhow, but by political and economic considerations. Space exploration can be expensive, and the two nations that led humanity into space—the United States and Soviet Union—have preferred to spend their money on earth-bound military objectives (it is also true that without the rivalry between these two nations, the moon missions might never have taken place).

If the world of the next millennium evolves as it might, with the danger of war receding and international cooperation grow-ing, money that might have been spent on war (or preparations for war) could be spent on space exploration instead.

If this is done, the profits to humanity would be enormous. It is all too often suggested that space exploration is nothing more than another case of pyramid building, another example of human *hubris* on a par with those tombs of the pharaohs.

However, this is a very bad analogy. The pyramids, except for their impressive evidence of what human beings can do with relatively primitive technology, served no real purpose. However, space exploration has already brought us enormous benefits.

In the previous chapter, we discussed the idea of the world as one. This awareness is due, to some extent, to the view of the whole earth from space, provided to us by the Apollo missions in particular. When we see the earth in that way, we realize that the borders and boundaries created by nations are not there in reality.

In addition, communications satellites have knit together all the continents and we can now see everything happening on Earth, almost as it happens. It was because Americans could watch the war in Vietnam on television that people grew disillu-sioned with it. It is because we can see what happens in Beijing and Johannesburg and Moscow and Washington, that govern-ments are increasingly unable to act against the common interest with impunity.

Navigation satellites have mapped the world more accurately and made sailing the seas far safer. Weather satellites pinpoint hurricanes and make it possible to prepare for them, saving hundreds or even thousands of lives each year. Remote sensing satellites allow us to study the earth's resources, its forests, grain fields, and its fisheries on a global scale. Even spy satellites are useful, because they make arms-control agreements possible. They also make it virtually impossible for nations to carry out clandestine military maneuvers.

So far, however, most of humanity's efforts in space have included only minimal direct human participation. Once we build a permanent space station and other permanent outposts, it will be possible to get serious about developing the space frontier. The Solar System is rich in resources, and access to extraterrestrial materials will be of the greatest importance. If a base is built on the moon, metals from its soil can be smelted. Oxygen can be obtained, and concrete and glass can be created.

Humans settle the solar system

Using materials from the moon, we can build vast structures in space, including space settlements, with a minimal drain on Earth's resources. Solar power satellites can be placed in orbit around the earth, absorbing the sun's radiation without interference by Earth's atmosphere, weather, or nightfall. If the various obstacles to such systems can be overcome, a given array of photoelectric cells will produce sixty times as much energy as could be obtained on the earth's surface.

We can build laboratories and observatories in space to vastly increase human knowledge, and factories will be built to make use of the special properties of outer space—zero gravity (microgravity), hard solar radiation, high and low temperatures, and unlimited vacuum. Devices and materials can be manufactured in space under such conditions that could only be produced with difficulty, if at all, on the earth.

In this way, some industrial plants can also be removed from the surface of the earth, where they are in intimate contact with our biosphere. These facilities can be placed in space, close enough to us to be of immediate use, but far enough away so that they cannot pollute the planet.

All of these things can be done while remaining within an area that we already have explored to some extent—the earth-moon system, or what is called cislunar space. This effort to explore and utilize cislunar space for the good of humanity will have many direct material benefits, but it will provide important indirect benefits, as well.

First, it will have the unifying effect of engaging all the earth in a vast project designed to benefit the entire planet. It will, for the first time in history, allow humanity to experience a truly common purpose. In particular, the development of a major energy source from solar power stations will give all nations the incentive to create an orderly and peaceful society on Earth. Disorders on Earth that might disrupt the steady maintenance of such stations would cut off the energy supply for everyone, and that would be in no one's interest. Just as international cooperation will make advances in space easier to carry out, so will advances in space development support continued international cooperation. The traditional hatreds and suspicions of the nations may begin to fade in the face of the common necessity of making space society workable.

Second, to keep the space-based society functioning, it will require that people are in space at all times. Settlements will be built, each capable of holding thousands of individuals. These space people may spend their entire lives in space, have children, grow old, and die there, without ever returning to Earth.

Their lives will be different from that of terrestrial humans in many ways, as different as farmers from hunters, or factory workers from shepherds. They will be accustomed to living inside a world, rather than on the outer surface as we do. For many of them, their world will actually be a large spaceship.

They will take for granted the entire experience of space travel, and they will also be ecology minded, living with recycled air, water, and food in a finite habitat. They will also be affected by circumstances of variable gravity, something that is almost impossible to experience on Earth.

Overall, they will be more suited psychologically to extended space voyages than Earth-people would be. The exploration and settlement of the far distant parts of the Solar System—Mars, the asteroids, and the satellites of Jupiter and Saturn—are probably going to be carried out by the early settlers of cislunar space and their descendants.

If we look back at human history, we see a restless species that has always explored and developed whatever "space" opened up to it. The human movement into outer space, while it will be an extraordinary enterprise, is not inconsistent with everything humans have done while on Earth. In some ways, nothing could be more logical than the human development of the space environment.

By the year 3000, then, it may well be that Earth will be only a small part of the human realm. It may still be the most populated part, and it will always be humanity's original home, but there will certainly be outposts throughout the Solar System, at the very least—clusters of human beings, each with its own world of plants and animals, carefully designed to maintain an ecological balance.

The foregoing predictions can be made with some degree of confidence because they reflect directions already being taken by human beings, and trends that have been in place for several millennia. It is difficult to say more, however, because so many variables might intervene that cannot be foreseen as human beings begin to explore space in a serious way.

For example, settling the Solar System is a task that can be accomplished within the limits of current technology, but leaving the Solar System is another matter altogether. The nearest star is four light-years away, which means that it would take four years traveling at the speed of light to get there. However, there will certainly be space pioneers who will want to migrate to the stars, and perhaps that process will have begun by the year 3000.

Thinking about travel to the stars brings to mind another possibility that holds even greater implications for the future of humanity, and that is contact with extraterrestrial intelligence. With some 200 to 400 billion stars in our galaxy alone, and billions of galaxies in the universe, there are many sites where life and intelligence may have evolved.

Even now, there are a number of private efforts under way to detect radio signals from extraterrestrial civilizations that might

be out there, and the National Aeronautics and Space Administra- *NASA plans to*
tion (NASA) plans to initiate its own project before we reach the *begin scientific*
year 2000.   *"search for*
                                                                   extraterrestrial
Our analysis of the development of human civilization over *intelligence"*
several millennia has included the intervention of many unexpected events, but nothing on the order of contact with extraterrestrial civilizations. Surely, this would be one of the most
important events of the next millennium if it did take place.

With or without contact, however, we can safely assume that
the human exploration of outer space will be a central factor in
the lives of our descendants in the coming millennium. Let's look
now at some other elements of the future.

THE DEVELOPMENT OF AGRICULTURE AND HERDING TEN *Computer*
thousand years ago had one deleterious side effect that is not *Technology*
often mentioned. It converted humans from being active
hunters who pitted their brains and skill against other animals
into passive tenders of animal herds and fields of grain. Agriculture, in particular, required hard and unremitting labor of a type
that never properly utilized the marvelous human brain, and it
was agriculture that occupied the vast majority of the human
species until the 1700s.

Until the 1700s, most human beings worked their muscles
endlessly and their brains rarely. Muscles atrophy if they are not
used, and so do mental and reasoning abilities. Throughout the
world, the peasants were scorned by those who did not have to
work the fields. The farm workers were considered by these
"aristocrats" to be little better than the beasts laboring alongside
them.

Those working the land did have their own kind of knowledge,
but it was limited to the immediate task at hand. The work
narrowed and specialized them, until eventually they could not
easily exercise their minds in other areas, even if they wanted to.

The industrial revolution began a process that ultimately freed
much of humanity from the necessity of hard, unskilled physical
labor, and it gave a larger proportion of the population a chance

to have an education. However, until around 1950, the nature of work in an industrialized society was still too often dull, repetitious, and stultifying. Most human beings still had no occasion to truly exercise their minds to any great extent, and those minds still atrophied, a problem that our educational system could not resolve.

Why, though, is it necessary for human beings to work at jobs, whether digging ditches or typing letters repetitively, that underuse and atrophy the human brain? The answer is that nothing less intricate than the human brain can perform the tasks, despite their mindless nature. Animals cannot substitute for humans in these tasks and neither could any machine developed before 1950. There was, therefore, no choice, and humans had to perform the tasks. The situation is comparable to chopping up mahogany furniture for firewood—it's not something that you want to do, but when a fire is absolutely required and no other fuel is available, you do it.

There have always been individuals, of course, who produce wonderful works of art and literature, science and philosophy, and are statesmen and leaders, as well. Our review of the millennia has revealed a few people of this type who appear in every era. These, however, are considered to be completely unrepresentative of humanity in general. They are considered exceptional, creative, thinking people, and the vast majority of the rest of us are just . . . well . . . peasants.

As we have also seen in our review of the past, however, technological innovation often transforms society and our view of what is possible. In the 1940s, a great change of this type took place with the invention of the electronic computer and the transistor. Over time, computers have been made smaller, cheaper, and enormously more powerful. By the mid-1970s, with the invention of the microchip, room-sized computers had been reduced to the desktop machines like the one on which this book is being written.

In the mid-1970s, then, it became possible for computers to enter the workplace on a large and affordable scale as devices that more closely mimicked the human brain than anything that had existed before, devices that could be relied upon to do work that only humans had done in the past. Moreover, computers could be used to guide mobile machines that we call robots.

In short, we are now well into a period in which computers and robots are able to do the dull, repetitive work that human beings have done for millennia; the kind of work that makes robots out of the human beings compelled to do it.

However, we must note that this era has only just begun. While computers and robots have taken over much of the repetitive work of society, they will do much more, especially as the field of artificial intelligence expands, and machines become "smarter."

Thus, the question arises: If we take these myriad nonhuman jobs and give them to computers and robots to perform, what are human beings going to do?

The obvious answer is that human beings will turn to *human* work, a kind of work that will draw upon the full power of the human brain. It is exactly the kind of work that has been done by "extraordinary individuals" in the past, and can be done by "mere mortals" in the future. Human beings can now begin to contribute on a vast scale to art and literature, science and engineering, philosophy and leadership. They can devise methods for controlling and directing robots, initiating new ways of using them to expand the frontiers of knowledge. Humans can, with the help of computers and robots, more rapidly expand into outer space and set up new types of civilizations, for example.

But then, you might ask, "How can human beings *en masse* indulge in all these creative activities? Surely very few of them are mentally equipped for such things."

However, this view is based on the distortions produced by the situations of an earlier era, when only a few people could break free to realize their full capabilities. This view completely underestimates human capacities, judging the human species as a whole and forever by the pathological conditions under which human beings have been forced until now to live.

This has, of course, happened before. In the preindustrial world, literacy was a property that belonged only to a very small group of human beings. Clerics, merchants, and artisans might be able to read and write, but the vast majority of human beings could not. It wasn't that they didn't have the capacity to learn; there simply was no reason for them to know how.

It was very easy to suppose that the ability to convert speech into a series of markings, and the ability to look at those markings and convert them into speech was a very unusual and creative ability that only a few human minds could master.

The advent of printing in 1450 changed all of that. Soon, there was a flood of reading material that made it more worthwhile for more people to become literate. Then, the industrial revolution brought a flood of people from the farms into the factories.

People who earlier would have tended growing grain now had to work with expensive machinery. It now became *necessary* for the new factory workers to be literate, if only so that they could read instructions and write simple reports. The industrial nations then set up free public schools and *compelled* children to attend.

And behold: It turned out that if children were given an opportunity to read and write, they would learn to do so, and today the percentage of people who are literate is enormously greater than it was in preindustrial times. Undoubtedly, the intellectuals of the world, even as late as 1750, would be flabbergasted if they could have known that two centuries later literacy would have become so common a phenomenon.

In the same way, what we call creativity today may turn out to be the common property of humanity, once the conditions of life are suitably changed. The most fundamental of the changes to be made, after the introduction of the computer and the robot into full partnership with humanity, is to revise the educational system.

Today, it is necessary for one teacher to teach many students at the same time, and this can only be done by following a fixed curriculum that applies to all the students. However, the students are individuals, and a fixed curriculum does not maximize the opportunity provided by their uniqueness.

Some of the students find the course of instruction too slow and become bored; some find it too fast and become confused; some find it moving in the wrong direction and become angry.

The system is structured so that no student can possibly be satisfied with his or her education.

However, what would happen if there were a computer in every home? What would happen if all the information in the libraries of the world were available to the person using that computer?

Children are curious. In fact, every human being is curious if their brains have not been stultified by lack of use. People *want* to know, because there is a three-pound, incredibly complex brain inside our skulls with mental creativity, as its overriding reason for existence, built into it.

It may seem that people do not want to learn, but that is because they have been worn down, first by mass schooling, and then by dull jobs. If people associate learning with drudgery, then, they will of course not want to learn. Who would? But suppose they are given a new and pleasant way to learn; *then* what would happen? This is an unprecedented idea that will be an essential question for the next millennium to answer.

What if, in addition to institutionalized schoolwork where a student can learn to interact with his or her peers and adults, there were also an opportunity to exercise curiosity, asking questions and finding out answers with the help of a competent, never-tiring personal computer? Imagine further that this computer is far in advance of what is available today, and has at its disposal all the knowledge of human civilization.

A student, learning what he or she *wants* to learn, at a self-determined pace, will surely find the process infinitely enjoyable. The more the youngster is left to himself in such matters, the better off he or she will be. The self-learning process may well begin with trivia, but the educational goals will eventually become more elaborate. Then, too, once children experience the joys and freedom of learning, why should they ever stop? People who enjoy golf or tennis continue to play these games as long as they are physically capable of doing so, and the joys of gaining knowledge are likely to be longer lived—brains properly utilized remain in good condition much longer than muscles do.

Children who love to learn will become adults who love to learn. If computers and robots are properly applied to the task of

Computers create a revolution in education and many other areas of life

teaching us, the world of the next millennium will become a place where creativity is far more common than it ever was in the past.

Is this an idealistic view of what might happen in the future, or is it a realistic possibility? We have already seen that once a new technology becomes available, its potential is often realized in ways that seem miraculous, not because of idealism but because of the practical benefits to society. Thus, the computer's ability to foster human creativity may well be utilized to its fullest, not because it would be a wonderful thing but because it will serve important social functions.

Moreover, we are already moving in the direction of making computers available to everyone for home use, while collecting the maximum amount of knowledge into data bases that can be freely accessed by anyone who wants to use them. Finally, computers are being used with mixed success in the educational system of today.

What is needed now is a vision of how all of these elements can be blended together to create the educational revolution that is surely possible with what is at hand. Perhaps someone with that vision will bring it to fruition in the next millennium; perhaps such a person is reading this book right now.

Of course, there are those who worry about computers and robots outpacing the human mind and making humanity obsolete. They fear that machines will replace us, but this completely underestimates the complexity of the human brain. The brain consists of 10 billion neurons and 90 billion supporting cells. These neurons are interlaced in an enormously complex fashion, with each cell hooked up to anywhere from ten to a thousand other cells. Finally, each cell is not a mere on-off switch, but is itself a complex web of millions of elaborate molecules whose functions are currently beyond our understanding.

It will be a very long time before computers can be built with even a fraction of the complexity of the human brain, and even if they do become that complex, the style of computerized perform-ance will still be very different from that of the human brain. Computers will be able to do things that humans cannot do, but we will still be able to do things they cannot. It will be a partnership, a case of human beings and computers representing two different types of intelligence, which can do far more together than either could do alone.

I N THE INTRODUCTION TO THIS BOOK, IT WAS SUGGESTED *A Positive* that an understanding of past millennia might help us to create *Future* a positive future for ourselves and our descendants in the next millennium. If this is so, how might we go about using the knowledge gained by our millennial review to think about affecting the next millennium for the better?

First, we have to admit that our five trends (population, energy, war, space, and computers) are only examples of the issues that should be on the next millennium's agenda. There are many other matters that must also be addressed by the people of the twenty-first century and beyond.

For example, everything that has been said so far confronts us with the inevitable conclusion that the environment must continue to receive serious attention. All the agenda items (even computers, which can be very useful in finding solutions to the problems we face) discussed in this chapter impinge on the environmental question, and addressing them intelligently will help to resolve the current crisis.

In fact, every major development by human civilization has environmental implications. As we have seen, Nature would hardly have noticed the presence of human beings on Earth in the earliest millennia. Through clever use of our brains and our resulting inventiveness, however, humans have become the dominant force on this planet. As human civilization has developed, it has brought many benefits to humanity, but at a great cost to the environment itself.

Going into outer space should not be seen as an occasion for ignoring our newfound ecological awareness. Humans have already created an incredible amount of debris in Earth's orbit, which will eventually have to be cleaned up. As we move outward into the Solar System, we will either take ecological thinking with us, or rediscover it when new problems arise out there.

A second matter that must receive attention lies in the realm of politics and economics. Looking back over the millennia, it seems apparent that one of the great struggles of human history has been between political systems that focus on authoritarian control of people's lives (dictatorships) and those that depend upon people being free in order to function at all (democracies).

After many centuries of conflict in which the issue always seemed in doubt, it now appears to be resolved in favor of democracy by people the world over. In most cases, this also appears to imply that a free market will be the order of the day in the economic domain.

However, there is another theme in human history over the millennia that is not necessarily resolved by this commitment to democratic government and free enterprise, and that is the conflict between the rich and the poor, the haves and the have-nots. These divisions persist in democratic societies, and they continue to divide the world today.

Racial divisions and ethnic strife, close relatives of class conflict, also persist as humanity prepares for the next millennium, and we will have to find a way to resolve these matters or manage them more effectively if a positive future is to be achieved.

In considering all of these questions, the people of the next millennium will be faced with one critical choice—whether to govern on a global basis or to keep governmental functions divided into the national and regional units that exist today. There are many arguments on both sides of this question, but it is another issue that cannot be ignored.

What we decide to do may not be as important as *how* our actions are determined. Looking back over the past shows that history is affected by individuals, and not just the rulers and kings. The philosophers, spiritual teachers, inventors, and even writers have, in the end, often wielded far more power than the emperors, kings, and even presidents.

We noted earlier that one advantage of population growth is that it increases the probability of brilliant and useful ideas being generated. Today, there are over 5 billion human beings on the planet, and more are on the way. Each person has the potential to create and share with the world an idea or invention that will change the course of history.

However, that will not happen unless we encourage our children, who are the people of the next millennium, to think expansively and offer their thoughts to others. Thus, creating a positive future begins with the belief that such a future is possible. It means having the perspective that humanity, for all the mistakes we have made, has come a long way since the dawn of civilization, and there is a long way yet to go.

If we approach our problems intelligently and take the trouble to solve them, the year 3000 may see humanity living in a world of stable population and ecological balance, with outposts throughout the solar system, each with its own culture. We may see a human civilization, on the whole, offering a richness and variety far beyond anything we now know.

The people of 3000 may live with secure, and essentially nonpolluting sources of energy that will last for billions of years (as long as the sun does), and they may live in a world that is finally at peace. What's more, they may be living in a world where the dull, nonhuman work will be done by machines, freeing humans to indulge in creative endeavors on a scale and with an intensity unimaginable today.

It could be a very good world, and the people of 3000 may look back on 2000 as the end of humanity's childhood, the time when it emerged into adolescence and began to advance at long last to the adulthood of the species.

INDEX